Michael Ots clearly connects with the

and 'tells it as it is', communicating biblical truth in a readily accessible way.

Rev. John D. Brand, Principal, Faith Mission Bible College, Edinburgh

If you struggle to believe that Christianity is good, beautiful and true, then read this book. Michael Ots will take you on a warm-hearted, humorous and engaging journey into the heart of the Christian message. It will probably make you want to believe Christianity is true and will also give you good reasons to do so.

Richard Cunningham, Director UCCF: The Christian Unions

Michael Ots has three great strengths. He is a brilliant apologist, a compelling evangelist and a gifted writer. This, his second book, is bang up to date on contemporary issues about the Christian faith and full of scintillating illustrations. Buy it, learn from it and give it to a friend!

Canon Dr Michael Green, apologist, author and speaker

This book really stood out to me because it provides a practical guide to some of the more pressing questions of Christianity. It is a well-written account of why being a Christian can be looked at from a rational and evidential viewpoint. Michael's ability to give practical real-life examples of his journey as a Christian is a must-read for people from all walks of life. This thought-provoking book will provide answers to many questions and will fundamentally challenge us to think about our own future.

Deacon Manu, international rugby captain

Michael Ots is a brilliant communicator. He takes the reader on an intriguing journey and tackles the heartfelt questions of our age with insight and humour. Anyone seeking after meaning and truth would do well to read this book.

Amy Orr-Ewing, UK Director, Oxford Centre for Christian Apologetics

What Kind of Hope? not only gives seekers hope that life has meaning and purpose – but Michael Ots gives us solid reasons why. He does so with such buoyancy and joy that it's immediately apparent why Christians are the most hopeful people on earth. This book is also great for believers who want to deepen their understanding of the gospel and to learn how best to present it, from a real pro!

Rebecca Manley Pippert, speaker and author of Out of the Salt Shaker *and* Hope Has Its Reasons

This brilliant book will take you on a journey. It offers a radical and different view of hope that makes sense, both in the philosophy seminar and in the doctor's waiting room, with the hilarious and incredibly well-read Michael Ots as your guide. He is a great communicator.

Tom Price, tutor and speaker at the Oxford Centre for Christian Apologetics and associate tutor at Wycliffe Hall, Oxford

This is like a holiday brochure of hope: sunny, inviting and a pleasure to read. It leaves you with a happy sense of yearning.

Michael Reeves, Head of Theology, UCCF; author of The Good God

Along with the vast majority of atheists and agnostics, Richard Dawkins, author of *The God Delusion*, believes that everyone is entitled to their own opinions, but that, as far as possible, their opinions should be informed by all of the available evidence. In this thought-provoking book, Michael Ots draws our attention to the eyewitness accounts of Jesus' resurrection, the truth claim on which Christianity is based. By doing so he shows us that Christianity may be more rational than many believe and highlights the need to review the evidence.

Victoria Wright, former Vice President of the Humanist, Atheist, Secularist and Agnostic Society at Liverpool University

To/ Claire & Andy,

WHAT KIND OF
HPE?

Thanks so much for your
encouragement + support!

Blessings,

Moby

WHAT KIND OF HOPE?

How Jesus
changes
everything

MICHAEL OTS

INTER-VARSITY PRESS
Norton Street, Nottingham NG7 3HR, England
Email: ivp@ivpbooks.com
Website: www.ivpbooks.com

First published 2012

British Library Cataloguing in Publication Data
A catalogue record for this book is available from the British Library.

ISBN: 978–1–84474–604–0

Set in Monotype Dante 12/15pt
Typeset in Great Britain by Servis Filmsetting Ltd, Stockport, Cheshire
Printed in Great Britain by Ashford Colour Press Ltd, Gosport, Hampshire

*Inter-Varsity Press publishes Christian books that are true to the Bible
and that communicate the gospel, develop discipleship and strengthen the
church for its mission in the world.*

*Inter-Varsity Press is closely linked with the Universities and Colleges
Christian Fellowship, a student movement connecting Christian Unions
in universities and colleges throughout Great Britain, and a member
movement of the International Fellowship of Evangelical Students.
Website: www.uccf.org.uk*

CONTENTS

ACKNOWLEDGMENTS

I had been a Christian for several years before I ever seriously thought about what the Bible had to say about the future. I'm deeply indebted to Trevor Pearce, whose teaching on this subject has changed my understanding of it ever since. Not only did I realize that the Christian vision of the future was far better than I had ever dared to hope, I also appreciated that it made all the difference to my life here and now.

Thank you so much to Chris and Sarah Warton for your kind hospitality as I wrote this book. I couldn't have hoped for a warmer welcome – or warmer weather! Cape Town is a wonderful place to write in January. Thank you too to those who helpfully read through the manuscript and made comments that have improved the book considerably: Thank you Dad, Mike Reeves, Mary Navey, Christine Dillon, Chris Oldfield (sorry I forgot to thank you last time!), Victoria Wright and Alex and Jess Holt (and thanks for being great neighbours as well!). It is a joy to work so closely with

UCCF; I have been greatly influenced and helped by their formal training and also informal friendships with many of the staff. Thank you to Eleanor Trotter, Emily Ettridge and Kath Stanton at IVP for your encouragement and help. Thank you Gaynor Brown for trying your hardest to organize my life and for your input into the book. I am blessed to work for MOET, a great organization with wonderfully supportive trustees. Thank you for encouraging me to write and giving me the time and space to do it.

Most of all I am thankful for my parents who first showed me the difference that hope can make, and to Iustina for loving me and giving me so much to hope for!

INTRODUCTION

It cost around $300 million and took fifteen years to make. Yet *Avatar* still didn't win an Oscar. It did though, unintentionally, achieve something else: Pandora Syndrome. So realistic was its 3D portrayal of the imaginary planet Pandora that many people felt like it was real. They found that they longed to be a part of such a world and felt depressed, in comparison, by the sad reality of ours.

You may not have suffered from Pandora Syndrome, yet deep down many of us are aware that there seems to be something wrong with this world. Confronted with the daily news as well as the circumstances of our lives, we can often feel that 'it shouldn't be this way'. We also find we have a longing for something better. A world that is free from the pain, suffering, injustice and death that are a daily reality in this one. But is that hope just a pipe dream?

Our problem is that we find we can become disillusioned by so many promises of hope that never materialize. Before

Barack Obama became president of the United States he published his book entitled *The Audacity of Hope*. His campaign slogan was the phrase 'Yes, we can!' Yet looking back, for many, the hopes have yet to be realized. The expectation was much greater than the realization. The American pop and blues musician John Mayer puts it well in his song 'Waiting on the World to Change'.[1] He laments the fact that we are all misunderstood and don't have a way to rise above what is happening and put it right – so we are waiting for the world to change. We are waiting, but will change ever come? Tired of empty promises and shattered dreams, we can become cynical about hope.

Hope and the Bible

The Bible too speaks about hope. Not just a hope that somehow an individual can survive death, but a hope that this whole world can be made new. It is this hope that we are going to discover together.

Of course it may well be that you are *especially* sceptical about what the Bible has to say about the future. And there may be several reasons why.

It might well seem that Christian views about the future are open to a lot of debate and speculation. You may also have been put off by eccentric Christians who are forever predicting the date of Christ's return and then have to predict it again when it doesn't happen. Some novels and movies go well beyond what the Bible says, giving the impression that Christians are a bunch of crackpots. As a result, it wouldn't be surprising if we tried to avoid this area of Christian teaching altogether.

And how do we know that this hope isn't also an illusion, a cruel mirage destined to disappoint us? Is it based on anything more than wishful thinking? How do we know that it will really deliver?

We may also feel that Christian hope is nothing more than escapism from the harsh realities of life. Christians have sometimes been accused of being 'too heavenly minded to be of any earthly use'. Shouldn't we just get on with life and make the best of what we have?

Why bother looking at what the Bible says about the future?

We can't avoid the future

If the Bible's claims about the future are true, then they will have implications for all of us. Those claims are so big that, even if there were just a small chance they were true, they would still be worth looking into. Most of the people who have rejected Christianity that I meet have not investigated it and found it unconvincing, but rather they have never really looked into it at all. You may, if you take the trouble, find the evidence more compelling than you expect.

The future affects how we feel

No matter how much we say we only live for the moment, the future will indeed affect how we feel. My feelings today will be affected (in different ways obviously!) if I know that tomorrow I am going to the dentist or going on holiday. In particular, having hope in the future can help us now when life is tough.

Imagine two people. They are both given exactly the same job for a year. They have to work eight hours a day for five days each week in a factory where they pack boxes. Neither gets any holidays and they only have half an hour for lunch. The first is told that at the end of the year he will have earned £10,000. The second is told that he will have earned £100,000,000! Do you think that will affect the way they go about their work? Of course! The first will drag himself out of bed and head begrudgingly to work. The second will jump out of bed and work with a smile on his face. Why? Because he has hope.[2]

The future affects how we live

The technical word that Christians use to talk about the future is 'eschatology'. It may sound rather weird and way-out but it's actually pretty simple. Just as archaeology is the study of beginnings (from the word *arche* meaning 'beginning') so eschatology is the study of how things end (from the word *eschaton* meaning 'ending'). Whoever we are, we all have an eschatology – some belief about the future that makes a difference to us now.

On a more practical level, imagine I know that in a year's time I am moving to a different part of the world. That knowledge changes me now – I will probably start to learn the language, learn about the country and get to know people who live there. The future affects how we live now.

> *The future affects how we live now.*

Three views about the future

Death is the end

But what if death *is* the end, if this material world is all there is and this life is the only one we are going to get? It would appear that this view of the future should cause us to live the fullest possible lives now, for if this life is all we have, then surely we should make the most of it – travel the world, have fun, enjoy sex and do as much as we can. There are many books advising us on 101 places to visit, things to do, and experiences to have before we die.

What if death really is the end? For a start, most of us are aware that life isn't nearly long enough to do all the things that we want to do. I remember halfway through my twenties realizing that, even if I wanted to, it was now too late to become a professional sportsman, no matter how hard I tried (with the exception perhaps of lawn bowls!). The opportunity had gone forever. I would love to study philosophy, history and several sciences. I want to learn to play the piano. I wish I could have a go at several careers, including being a photographer, an architect, a farmer and graphic designer. I wish I could travel to other countries, not just for a week or two but long enough to learn the language and understand the culture. There are so many things I would love to do, but I realize that no matter how hard I try I'll never be able to do them all. I find I have eternity in my heart but only seventy or so years in my body.

I'm also left wondering what is the point of all that I do manage to achieve. What will become of all my learning, my experiences and my relationships? Nothing ultimately lasts. I remember once being asked if I knew the names of my great grandparents. I realized to my surprise that I didn't even know the name of either of my grandfathers, as they had both died before I was born. It was a sobering thought to contemplate that within two or three generations I too would probably be forgotten.

The artist Francis Bacon put it this way: 'Man now realizes that he is an accident, that he's a completely futile being . . .'[3]

In his book *A Free Man's Worship*, Bertrand Russell spoke openly of the implications of living in a purely materialistic world:

Man is the product of causes which had no prevision of the end they were achieving; that his origin, his growth, his hopes and

fears, his loves and his beliefs, are but the outcome of accidental
collocations of atoms . . . all the labours of the ages, all the
devotion, all the inspiration, all the noonday brightness of human
genius, are destined to extinction in the vast death of the solar
system, and that the whole temple of man's achievement must
inevitably be buried beneath the debris of a universe in ruins
. . . Only within the scaffolding of these truths, only on the
firm foundation of unyielding despair, can the soul's habitation
henceforth be safely built.[4]

I respect Russell's consistency. He very honestly portrays
the bleak reality of a world without God and without hope.
But even he struggled to live with it. Later on he admitted,
'The centre of me is always and eternally a terrible pain – a
curious wild pain – a searching for something beyond what
the world contains.'[5]

In his song 'Black and Gold', the Australian singer and
songwriter Sam Sparro admits to a similar kind of fear:

'Cause if you're not really here
Then the stars don't even matter
Now I'm filled to the top with fear
But it's all just a bunch of matter.

I feel a way of something beyond them
I don't see what I can feel
If vision is the only validation
Then most of my life isn't real.[6]

Are we honestly content to live, knowing that most of the
things that are so valuable to us aren't even real? Can we live
meaningfully when we know that none of it actually counts
for anything in the end?

We disappear to paradise

Of course not everyone believes that death is the end. Some think that in the end we leave this world and go to some sort of spiritual paradise, or that after many cycles of reincarnation we eventually achieve nirvana. This may appear to offer some kind of hope. But if this is the case, then I may see involvement in this real physical world as a distraction at best. Why bother getting involved if my real home is elsewhere? Why look after the environment if this world is going to burn up? Why try to make the world a better place if it is doomed to destruction? Even worse, we may stand back and not try to alleviate suffering, if we think that the suffering is a punishment for some past life or a purification for a future one.

There's a different way

You may think that Christianity fits into this second category – we will eventually leave this world and head for heaven. It's certainly what some Christians seem to think, and the implications are obvious. One American politician quipped, 'We don't have to protect the environment; the second coming [of Jesus] is at hand.'[7]

However, the Christian view is unique. The Bible insists that death is not the end and there is more to come, yet this future hope doesn't lead to us living lives detached from this present world. That's because Christian hope is quite different from what we often expect, as we will soon discover.

Hope that makes a difference

On 28 August 1963, Martin Luther King stood on the steps of the Lincoln Memorial in Washington DC and delivered what became one of the most famous speeches in history. Just reading the transcript stirs my emotions today. He had a dream of what his country could become – a dream of a country freed from the institutionalized racism that dominated it at the time. How incredible must it have seemed in those days that a black person could ever become president of the United States?

What was it that motivated him? At the end of the speech he moved beyond his immediate hope for America and spoke of his ultimate hope for the world. His voice rang out: 'We will be able to speed up that day when *all* God's children . . . will be able to join hands and sing in the words of the old Negro spiritual: "Free at last! Free at last! Thank God almighty, we're free at last!".' It was his conviction that a final day of freedom was coming that drove him to work for freedom there and then. Christian hope doesn't lead to passivity in the face of a broken, divided world. It inspires action.

So what does the Bible say about the future? What evidence is there that this is true? If our beliefs influence our actions now, then what difference does the biblical view make? You may be surprised by what follows.

In chapter 1 we will look at the radical nature of Christian hope and see what it means for the future of our world. Then we will go back and see what went wrong with this world and what needs to be put right. In chapters 3 to 5 we will go 'back to the future' and see how Jesus gives us a glimpse of what that future will be like. Then we will see how this future world can be possible and how hope is more than just an illusion but rather based on objective evidence. Then finally, in chapters 8 and 9, we will think about what this means for our lives now.

This is an amazing hope, so amazing in fact that I can't wait for you to discover and enjoy it for yourself.

1. WHAT ARE YOU WAITING FOR?

'What do you think it's like?' asks Thomas J. in the classic film *My Girl*.

'What?' asks Vada.

'Heaven.'

Vada thinks for a minute and then muses, 'I think . . . everybody gets their own white horse and all they do is ride them and eat marshmallows all day. And everybody's best friends with everyone else. When you play sports, there's no teams, so nobody gets picked last.'

'But what if you're afraid to ride horses?' asks Thomas J.

'Doesn't matter . . . 'cause they're not regular horses. They've got wings. And it's no big deal if you fall 'cause you'll just land in a cloud.'

What's heaven *not* like?
Many people's concept of heaven, if they have one at all, is rather cloudlike and fluffy. It may sound quite nice in a film

like *My Girl*, but, compared to the physical realities of this life, it does sound rather unreal and, quite frankly, rather boring too.

In an episode of *The Simpsons*, Homer is given a guided tour around heaven while standing on a cloud. Along with a water slide and a pedicure, he's offered anything he wishes for. This may sound more appealing than winged horses but it still seems totally unreal.

These rather fluffy ideas of heaven are not confined to films and TV. Look at some Christian art and it would appear that the choice at the end of life is between being burned alive or attending an eternal church service. To most normal people, neither option is particularly appealing!

Even Christmas carols have got in on the act. Speaking about heaven, the end of one famous carol contains the lines:

> Where like stars His children crowned
> All in white shall wait around.[1]

Heaven has just become the staff canteen at the local hospital.

Whatever way we put it, the idea of eternal choir practice on a cotton-wool cloud, dressed in white pyjamas and surrounded by harp-strumming cherubs, doesn't do it for many of us.

Now it's worth noting that a lot of our imagery of heaven has little to do with what the Bible says. But even taking that into account, I want to let you into a secret . . .

I'm hoping not to go to heaven.

No, that wasn't a mistake. I'm really hoping that I don't have to go there.

It's not that I don't believe that heaven exists. I do. Nor is it because I think heaven will be as dull as in the examples I have just given. It won't be. But I'm hoping not to have to go there because it's not the final destination.

Heaven – not our final destination

I have flown to Romania many times. On some of my first trips I flew via Amsterdam. I was always excited as I set off from Heathrow, but that wasn't because I was going to Schiphol Airport! That was just the stopover. I was looking forward to getting to Romania, breathing the mountain air and seeing my friends.

The Bible never says that this heaven is our final destination. The Bible does say that those who die now may go to heaven but this is just a stopover. It's a much nicer stopover than Schiphol Airport, but the best is yet to come. Our final destination is actually much closer to home. We see this in the Bible passage below.

But is the Bible true?

Before we go further, I am aware that you may not think that the Bible is even true, let alone relevant. Don't stop reading though. The fact is that most of the people I have met who think this have never really read the Bible as an adult. If you haven't done so, then for the sake of intellectual credibility it would be worth knowing exactly what you have rejected! It may even be that the reason why you have rejected the Bible is that you don't *want* it to be true. You think of it as an out-of-date rulebook designed to spoil your enjoyment of life. If that's what you think, then please keep reading because I reckon you will be pleasantly surprised.[2]

The following passage comes from a book of the Bible called Romans. It is a letter written by an early Christian leader called Paul to a group of Christians in the city of Rome. In it he explains some of the core teaching of Christianity:

I consider that our present sufferings are not worth comparing with the glory that will be revealed in us. For the creation waits in eager expectation for the children of God to be revealed. For the creation was subjected to frustration, not by its own choice, but by the will of the one who subjected it, in hope that the creation itself will be liberated from its bondage to decay and brought into the freedom and glory of the children of God.

We know that the whole creation has been groaning as in the pains of childbirth right up to the present time. Not only so, but we ourselves, who have the firstfruits of the Spirit, groan inwardly as we wait eagerly for our adoption to sonship, the redemption of our bodies. For in this hope we were saved. But hope that is seen is no hope at all. Who hopes for what they already have? But if we hope for what we do not yet have, we wait for it patiently.[3]

Groaning

Some of the concepts in this passage may appear rather strange to us, but twice we read of something that is familiar: groaning. This isn't to be confused with moaning, nor is it to do with our reaction to bad jokes. Groaning is what we do when words are inadequate to express our sense of frustration or pain.

We are told that the whole of creation groans and that it was 'subjected to frustration'. Something has gone badly wrong with the cosmos. It's true that sometimes the world seems a wonderful place to live in, but at other times it can be the exact opposite. Tsunamis, earthquakes, droughts, famines, hurricanes and flooding are tragically all part of our world today.

But it's not just creation that is described as groaning. Romans also says that we groan too. Our bodies are amazing things. The human eye alone is staggering in its intricate detail and far more complex than even the best digital camera. But, though they are wonderful, our bodies are also weak and fragile. They get sick, broken and fatigued. They are susceptible to disease. Bits start to wear out and have to be replaced. In fact an old friend of mine (in both senses of the word) has had so many parts of his body replaced that he's not sure what's original any more! Ultimately, all of us will die. At times we can be all too well aware of our own fragility and mortality.

So in the face of a broken world and broken bodies, what is the hope that the Bible offers? What would you expect? Most of us naturally think that it would be to leave our existing bodies and this world and float off to a cloud called 'heaven' to live a bodiless existence.

But we'd be wrong.

That may be what *The Simpsons* says. It may be what *My Girl* says. It may even be what many Christians have said in the past. But it's not what the Bible says. So what exactly does it say?

New bodies

A friend of mine told me how, when films are translated into other languages, the titles sometimes get distorted. One version of *The Shawshank Redemption* got called *The Shawshank Escape*. It tended to ruin the ending somewhat! 'Redemption' sounds to us like a religious word. But really it is quite simple. It is to do with being set free, just as the film portrays. In biblical times a slave could be redeemed and set free from captivity. Paul says that 'we wait . . . for . . . the redemption of our bodies'. Notice that he doesn't say redemption *from* our bodies. We might think that our hope is to be set free from these decaying bodies to live a non-physical existence. But it's quite the opposite – the hope is that these bodies will be set free from what causes them to decay.

When I think of redemption, I remember my failed attempts at baking as a boy. I would try to follow the recipe book and do everything right, but invariably I'd muck something up along the way. I'd end up with a whole load of ingredients mixed into what looked like an unappetizing slop. I'd be about to throw it away and start again when my mum would come to the rescue. Rather than chucking away the valuable ingredients, she would redeem them – by adding a bit of this or that, she'd make something new out of the mess I had made.

Christian hope is not for the rejection of our physical bodies but their redemption. God is not going to throw away this world but redeem and make it good again. This is very different from other religious and philosophical systems. For instance, the Buddhist hope is to escape the endless cycle of reincarnation and cease to be a physical being. In Greek thought there was a strong divide between the physical and the spiritual. The body was evil but the soul good. This idea influenced an early sect of Christianity called the Gnostics who also thought that the body was bad.

The reality is that, far from rejecting the physical world, the Bible embraces and endorses it. God created a physical world and declared that it was good. But even more than that, right at the centre of the Bible there is the claim that God himself became physical. In the person of Jesus, God didn't just take on the appearance of humanity – he became fully human and lived on planet earth. God stepped into space and time.

Jesus – our prototype

The biggest clue as to what happens to Christians after death is what happened to Jesus after his. We're told that Jesus is like a prototype, an example of what will happen to all who trust in him.[4] Jesus didn't rise from death simply as a ghost or a disembodied soul. He had a body. It could be seen, touched, hugged and heard. He ate food like a regular human being. His body was in some ways the same as it had been – he was recognizable.[5] Yet in other ways it was different. He wasn't just a resuscitated corpse in need of medical treatment. His followers were convinced he had conquered death, never to die again.

Now you may not be convinced that Jesus' resurrection actually happened. (We'll think more about that in chapter 7.) But do you see the significance of it all if it did? If this is true, then Christian hope is not about leaving our bodies but getting new ones. These same bodies but set free from sickness, pain, decay and death. This existing body transformed and made new.

And this isn't just an interesting idea. It can bring incredible hope, especially to those who are only too well aware of the weaknesses of their bodies now. Take for example Joni Eareckson Tada who, after a diving accident in her teens, has spent decades as a quadriplegic. She writes,

> I still can hardly believe it. I, with shrivelled, bent fingers, atrophied muscles, gnarled knees, and no feeling from the shoulders down, will one day have a new body, light, bright, and clothed in righteousness – powerful and dazzling. Can you imagine the hope this gives someone spinal cord-injured like me? Or someone who is cerebral-palsied, brain-injured, or who has multiple sclerosis? . . . No other religion, no other philosophy promises new bodies, hearts, and minds. Only in

the Gospel of Christ do hurting people find such incredible
hope.[6]

This amazing hope can affect all of us. All of us care about
our bodies. We want to stay healthy and look good. We
might imagine that the Bible says that this is a bad thing –
that we should be concerned only for the 'inner soul'. But
Christian hope is not about the rejection of our bodies but
the redemption of them. The Bible affirms that our physical bodies, far from being evil as some early Christian sects
believed, are good. It is not so much that we have a soul, but
we *are* a soul. So we should care about our bodies, and it is
perfectly natural to care about how we look.

Our problem is not that we care too much about our
bodies but that we don't care enough. We are content to
place our hopes in Nivea or Oil of Olay which, despite the
advertising claims, are severely limited in their powers!
They may keep us looking younger for a few more years but
not forever. The hope of the Bible is that these bodies can
one day be made new. If we really care about our bodies,
then we should be seriously interested in what the Bible has
to say.

A new world

Christian hope is not about leaving our bodies, but ultimately getting new ones. If heaven was about sitting on a
cloud, then we'd have a problem. We'd fall through! Real
bodies need a real world to live in, real food to eat and real
things to do.

Many Christians have mistakenly thought that our world
is waiting to be destroyed and that God will take people
away to heaven. (Often the reason behind this is a certain
passage in the New Testament: 2 Peter 3. For an explanation

of why I don't think this is the case, see the appendix.) But that would be quite different from what we read in this part of the Bible. We read that all creation is longing to be set free. And if being set free means being blowtorched into oblivion, then that would seem a very strange type of freedom indeed! God is not going to destroy the world, but transform it, with all that causes decay, destruction and death taken away.

Elsewhere the Bible talks about there being a 'new heaven and a new earth'.[7] That would seem to imply that this old world will end. But there are two ways in which you get something new. You may get a new car, in which case you sell or scrap your old one and get a brand new one. Nothing of the old car remains (except perhaps the fluffy dice hanging from the rear-view mirror). Or you might get a new kitchen installed. It would also be new, but in a different kind of way. For example, it is still the same room. There may even be some good parts of the old kitchen that are kept. But it is renewed. You rip out the rubbish and make it better. That is the way in which the Bible speaks about a new world. It's not that God gets rid of the old one and starts again, but that he renews and transforms it. However, just in case you're worried, I can assure you that it will be a whole lot more exciting than a new kitchen!

C. S. Lewis was an atheist before becoming a Christian through the influence of fellow Oxford University professor J. R. R. Tolkien. He used his brilliant imagination and liter-ary skill to capture this biblical idea in his famous children's stories that formed *The Chronicles of Narnia*. In the final book of the series, *The Last Battle*, the children have gone from Narnia into a new world and they are discussing where they think they are.

'If you ask me,' said Edmund, 'it's like somewhere in the Narnian world. Look at those mountains ahead . . . surely they're rather like the mountains we used to see from Narnia . . .?'

'Yes, so they are,' said Peter. 'Only these are bigger.'

'[And] those hills,' said Lucy, '. . . aren't they very like the Southern border of Narnia?"

'Like!' cried Edmund after a moment's silence. 'Why, they're exactly like . . .'

'And yet they're not like,' said Lucy. 'They're different. They have more colours on them and they look further away than I remembered and they're more . . . more . . . oh, I don't know . . .'

'More like the real thing,' said the Lord Digory softly.

Suddenly Farsight the Eagle spread his wings, soared thirty or forty feet up into the air, circled round and then alighted on the ground.

'Kings and Queens,' he cried, 'we have all been blind. We are only beginning to see where we are. From up there I have seen it all . . . Narnia is not dead. This is Narnia.'[8]

The new world that the children have entered is actually the same as the world they have just come from – just better and more real than the old one ever was. Our problem is that this world seems real and the future seems fluffy. But Lewis shows that, far from being less real, the world to come will be even more so. He goes on to say,

It is hard to explain how this sunlit land was different from the old Narnia . . . Perhaps you will get some idea of it if you think like this. You may have been in a room where there was a window that looked out on a lovely bay of the sea or a green valley that wound among the mountains. And in the wall of the room opposite to the window there may have been a [mirror]. And as you turned away from the window you suddenly caught

sight of that sea or that valley, all over again, in the [mirror]. And
the sea in the mirror, or the valley in the mirror, were in one
sense just the same as the real ones: yet at the same time they
were somehow different – deeper, more wonderful, more like
places in a story; in a story you have never heard but very much
want to know. The difference between the old Narnia and the
new Narnia was like that. The new one was a deeper country:
every rock and flower and blade of grass looked as if it meant
more. I can't describe it any better than that: if you ever get there
you will know what I mean.[9]

God's plan is so much bigger than taking a few people to
heaven. It is about the whole universe being made new and
set free. It is so much better than we think.

Vinoth Ramachandra, from Sri Lanka, put it this way:

> Our salvation lies not in an escape from this world but in the
> transformation of this world. Everything good and true and
> beautiful in history is not lost forever but will be restored and
> directed to the worship of God. All our human activity (in the
> arts and sciences, economics and politics) and even the nonhuman
> creation will be brought to share in the liberating rule of God. This
> grand vision centres on the cross of Jesus Christ. There a vision of
> future hope opens up for the world. You will not find hope for the
> world in any religious systems or philosophies of humankind. The
> biblical vision is unique. That is why when some say that there is
> salvation in other faiths I ask them, 'What salvation are you talking
> about?' No faith holds out a promise of eternal salvation for the
> world the way the cross and resurrection of Jesus do.[10]

Life-transforming hope

Having this kind of hope could totally transform your life
– now. We can enjoy this world fully when we realize that

it is a good gift to us from a loving God. God is as happy when I am cycling my bike across Europe or windsurfing across Poole Harbour as he is when I am reading my Bible or singing a Christian song. The physical world and these physical bodies are good, and they are designed to be enjoyed. So I will go and hike up mountains and go on crazy cycle rides. I'll enjoy meals with friends and holidays by the sea. And I'll enjoy them all the more, knowing that now is not the only chance I have to enjoy them.

Many of us frantically live life, trying to cram in as much as we can before we get too old to enjoy it. But if the Christian story is true, then there is no reason why I need to do everything before I die. In the new world that God makes, nothing good will be lost; in fact good things will be even better! All that is good about this world will be redeemed. We won't miss out.

Of course, it may be that you can't enjoy life now in the way it was intended. For you, the thought of enjoying life *at all* seems very distant and just getting through each day is a challenge in itself. For some people, it is not so much that they experience moments of pain, but that their whole life is made up of it. We are often all too conscious that it's not just the world but also our own bodies that are broken and don't work the way they should. This is where the Christian hope is so amazing. It is not simply that we will one day get a consolation prize to make up for the bad stuff now, but that the best is yet to come. With bodies set free from pain and suffering, we can enjoy a world that is also set free from all that once spoiled it.

I love *The Lord of the Rings*. I must admit that I had watched the films several times before I actually got round to reading the books. My favourite moment comes at the end of the second film, *The Two Towers*. Frodo feels like giving up.

Darkness is gathering, and it seems like evil will win. Then Sam (my favourite character) turns to Frodo and says,

> It's like in the great stories, Mr Frodo. The ones that really mattered. Full of darkness and danger, they were. And sometimes you didn't want to know the end. Because how could the end be happy? How could the world go back to the way it was when so much bad had happened? But in the end, it's only a passing thing, this shadow. Even darkness must pass. A new day will come. And when the sun shines it will shine out the clearer. Those were the stories that stayed with you. That meant something, even if you were too small to understand why.[11]

I think something of Tolkien's Christian faith comes through in what Sam says. His hope is not just for the world to go back to the way it was, but that it will be even better. It is the same hope that we encountered above in the letter to the Romans, where Paul writes, 'I consider that our present sufferings are not worth comparing with the glory that will be revealed in us.'[12] What we have to look forward to is so overwhelmingly good, it is beyond comparison.

What we have to look forward to is so overwhelmingly good, it is beyond comparison.

Shortly we will start to unpack what this will be like but, before we can know how the world will be put right, we need to ask first, 'What has gone wrong?'

2. WHAT'S WRONG WITH THIS WORLD?

It had been a wonderful day. I had spent it skiing with friends. Overnight snow had given way to clear blue skies revealing snow-capped mountains as far as the eye could see. Sun glinted off the snow-covered pine trees as we sped down the almost-deserted slopes, making fresh tracks as we went. The world had rarely felt like a more wonderful place.

It was only later, after we had eaten dinner and were sitting back to relax for the evening, that we first heard about it. A massive tsunami in Japan had left over 15,000 people dead. Fear of a nuclear meltdown was spreading. The news reports revealed the full extent of the devastation. We sat speechless as we watched the pictures of a wall of black water sweeping ships inland and wiping out everything in its path. In one day we had experienced nature as a beautiful friend, while to thousands of others it had been an ugly foe.

What a world of contrasts. A world filled both with breathtaking beauty and unspeakable suffering. However, it is not just in the natural world that such a paradox exists, but also within humanity itself. As human beings we have the capacity for so much love, creativity and goodness, as well as so much hate, destruction and evil. History has played host to individuals like Mother Teresa, Martin Luther King and Mahatma Gandhi, as well as Adolf Hitler, Pol Pot and Idi Amin. But it is not as simple as dividing the world into the good and the bad. The writer Aleksandr Solzhenitsyn put it this way:

> If only it were all so simple! If only there were evil people somewhere insidiously committing evil deeds, and it were necessary only to separate them from the rest of us and destroy them. But the line dividing good and evil cuts through the heart of every human being. And who is willing to destroy a piece of his own heart?[1]

We live in a world of good and evil, but we too are capable of both. How are we to make sense of such a world?

Why is our world so paradoxical?

Before studying for my degree, I took a gap year. Unlike some of my friends who hiked through jungles in South America, I went for the less exciting option and got a job at a large shop in the centre of my town! I was placed in the worst part of the store – the customer service desk. And the worst time was just after Christmas. Day after day I was faced with a queue of angry parents, bringing back faulty toys and demanding a refund. My manager told me I had to make a simple decision in each case. Was the item broken because of a manufacturing fault? Or was it misuse by the owner that was to blame?

The same question is a good one to ask when it comes to

our world. Are the problems the result of a manufacturing fault on the part of God or misuse by the people who have been left in charge?

Are the problems the result of a manufacturing fault on the part of God or misuse by the people who have been left in charge?

The first three chapters of the Bible help us to answer that question. Of course, these chapters have also been the focus of a lot of debate. Among Christians there are differences of interpretation over exactly how they should be read – literally or poetically.[2] But that doesn't stop them from agreeing on the core idea – that God made the world and something has gone wrong.

Whatever you think about how literally you should take these early chapters of the Bible, it is worth considering: does any other philosophy make so much sense of the world and our experience of it?

A good world

A recurring theme in the first chapter of the Bible is that God made the world, and he made it good. After each stage of creation, God declared that 'it was good'. Just in case we haven't got the point, after finishing his work of creation, God looked back over it all and said that 'it was very good' – bold, italic and underlined. What made it so good?

Relationship to our environment

The picture is one of nature in complete harmony. The world is a loving gift for human beings to enjoy, cultivate and look after. We are to exercise control over creation, but are to do so in a caring and productive way. We have work to do in the world, but that work is satisfying and good, part of what gives us significance and meaning. While we may complain about our jobs, and sometimes for good reason, work itself is an inherently good thing.

Relationships with others

Not only do we humans enjoy the world in which we live, but we also enjoy one another perfectly. We are told that 'it is not good for the man to be alone'.[3] Humans find joy not simply in relating to God in some kind of monastic separation, but we are to find it in our relationships with other people too. These relationships are incredibly satisfying, selflessly concerned with how we can serve and love the other person and at the same time find the other person acting in the same way towards us. Writing in the *Daily Telegraph*, psychologist Dr Cliff Arnall says,

> The most important thing in our lives are our relationships – and no amount of money can buy that. I've spoken to miserable multimillionaires and people who have no money but are very happy because they have amazing friends. Any psychologist, life coach or happiness expert will tell you that relationships with people are what makes you happy.[4]

Relationship with God

Though human beings are created by God, we can also enjoy a relationship with him. This is also quite different from many of our perceptions of how we might relate to God. We tend to imagine the relationship like that of a slave to a master or a subject to a dictator. In the Genesis account humans are pictured walking and talking with God in the garden during the evening,[5] just as friends might talk while walking through a park.

No pain and death

Nothing can spoil this world of wonderful relationships. There's no fear of sickness or death, no fear that it will come to an end. Only amazing relationships in a good world, enjoyed with healthy bodies that always work the way they should.

It all seems so good . . . but not for long. Just three chapters into the Bible and it all goes pear (or apple?) shaped.

The day that changed the world

Now the snake . . . said to the woman, 'Did God really say, "You must not eat from any tree in the garden"?'

The woman said to the snake, 'We may eat fruit from the trees in the garden, but God did say, "You must not eat fruit from the tree that is in the middle of the garden, and you must not touch it, or you will die."'

'You will not certainly die,' the snake said to the woman. 'For God knows that when you eat from it your eyes will be opened, and you will be like God, knowing good and evil.'

. . . She took some and ate it. She also gave some to her husband, who was with her, and he ate it. Then the eyes of both of them were opened, and they realised that they were naked; so they sewed fig leaves together and made coverings for themselves.

Then the man and his wife heard the sound of the LORD God as he was walking in the garden in the cool of the day, and they hid from the LORD God among the trees of the garden. But the LORD God called to the man, 'Where are you?'[6]

There is a story of an Englishman, a Frenchman and a Russian who were all looking at a painting depicting the events of the above passage. The Englishman spoke first. 'They're clearly English,' he pointed out in a posh accent. 'You see, she has only got one apple and she is giving it to him to eat.'

'*Non, non, non*,' interrupted the Frenchman. 'They are French. They are naked, and in a garden, eating fruit together.'

'*Nyet, nyet*,' objected the Russian. 'They must be Russian. Don't you see? They have hardly anything to eat, nothing to wear and yet they think they are in paradise!'

The whole idea of a talking snake tempting a naked couple to eat forbidden fruit in a paradise garden can seem like a bit of a joke. But the reality behind this is no joke. Many people said 9/11 was the day that changed the world. Actually, the claim of the Bible is that the day that changed the world happened much earlier. September 11 was simply another day that showed us what the world was really like. But what's the big deal about eating fruit?

Back in Genesis chapter 2, God had clearly said that there was only one thing that was off limits: the fruit of one tree. Everything else was to be enjoyed except this. To eat from that tree would result in death. So why would God create this possibility for disaster and put the tree there in the first place?

Imagine I meet a woman whom I find stunningly beautiful. I fall madly in love with her and eventually get down on one knee before her. However, rather than asking, 'Will you marry me?' I say, 'You will marry me!' Then I continue, 'When you marry me, you will cook me steak on Mondays and curry on Tuesdays, watch football with me on Wednesdays and do the washing on Thursdays.'

If this were my attitude, then it would be surprising if anyone agreed to marry me at all. That's not love. It's not that people in love never cook meals or do the washing for each other. But for it to be love, those actions must be free choices.

God wants people to live in loving relationship with him. But for that to be real, there has to be the possibility that people could choose to do the opposite. The tragedy is that people took that freedom and used it to reject God and go their own ways. Eating fruit may seem like a petty thing, but the more fundamental issue is not what they are doing but against whom they are doing it. Or imagine this: I get a cold call from a double-glazing salesman. Now I may be forgiven for hanging up on him in the middle of the call, especially if I am having my dinner. But imagine I do the same thing to my mum when she rings. The same action would be much more offensive because of who it is that I am rejecting. By eating the fruit, the original human beings were not just breaking a random rule, but rejecting the loving God who had given them everything they had.

Before we are too quick to condemn them for being so stupid, we need to stop and realize that in varying ways we have all done the same thing. You may or may not believe in God. But what if he does exist and we have spent our lives in his world, enjoying his gifts, and yet we reject or ignore him? That would be really serious.

So what were the consequences of this rejection?

A broken world

A broken relationship with our environment

The consequences of this one event spill over into the whole created order. A computer virus can start with one dodgy email and then infiltrate every aspect of the machine. In the same way, from this one event, sin has affected the whole cosmos. We see that living in the world is now going to be a battle. Thorns and thistles make farming a continual challenge. Work, which was in itself a good and satisfying thing, can often now be frustrating and difficult. Nature, which used to be a friend, is very often an enemy. Not many of us are farmers, but all of us can experience something of this frustration in our own work.

A broken relationship with others

The first thing that the man and woman notice after eating the fruit is that they are both naked. This may seem rather strange. Why hadn't they noticed it before?

Have you ever been shown a photo of a group of people, including you? Who is the first person you instinctively look at? Is it not usually yourself? We are often most conscious and worried about ourselves. Yet imagine a world where people didn't instinctively look at themselves. Where people were so other-centred that they had no thought for themselves at all. That was the kind of world God had made, but it has now been broken. From being other-conscious, the man and woman are now self-conscious. Rather than thinking about the other person, they are now only thinking about themselves.

They also engage in blaming each other. As one person put it, 'Adam blamed Eve, Eve blamed the serpent, and the serpent didn't have a leg to stand on!' Relationships that were once characterized by selfless love are now marred by guilt, blame-shifting and self-absorption. Not only does the man blame the woman, but he also blames God for giving her to him in the first place.[7]

Now whatever you think of this story, it's not hard to see that this is, sadly, a very accurate description of many of our relationships. Why do we end up hurting and getting hurt by those we are meant to love? Why do we long for love, but so often end up feeling used by others? Why can we be so quick to accuse and so slow to admit when we're wrong? It is not just the bombs of a terrorist that can hurt us, but also the words of those who were meant to be our friends.

A broken relationship with God

A woman phoned her friend and was surprised to hear her friend's four-year-old daughter answer in a hushed whisper.

'Can I speak to your mother?' she asked.

'No,' came the whispered reply. 'She's busy.'

'Oh well, is your father there?'

'Yes, but he's busy too,' she responded.

'Is anyone else there?' asked the now-confused woman.

'Yes – the police are here,' the little girl whispered.

'Can I speak with them then?'

'No, they're busy too.'

'Well, is anyone else there?' the friend asked, increasingly concerned.

'Yes, the fire brigade are here.'

'Well, can I speak with them?'

'No, they're busy too!'

Exasperated, the woman finally asked, 'So your mother and father are there, along with the police and the fire brigade, and they're all busy! What are they all doing?'

Without hesitation, back came the whispered reply: 'They're looking for me!'

We can smile at the thought of a little girl hiding with the phone while everyone else is searching for her. But ever since the events that we have just looked at, we too have been doing the same thing – hiding from God. Rather than running to God when they hear him walking in the garden, the first humans run away and hide. Love is replaced by fear. Rather than enjoying a close relationship, we see that they find themselves excluded and cut off. This ends up becoming our experience too. Many people can question the existence of God because he seems distant, but the reality is there is something significant that separates us from him.

In the centre of my home town of Bournemouth there is a large tethered balloon. Tourists can pay to stand in a cage suspended beneath it. They are rewarded with a great aerial view of the town as the balloon is released several hundred feet into the air. From my old flat I could see the balloon and would often watch it going up and down when I was supposed to be studying. I remember one such afternoon when I glanced out of the window to see where the balloon was. I looked up and it wasn't in the sky, and then I looked down and it wasn't on the ground. The cable was still there, but then it seemingly stopped in mid air. My heart missed a beat. Suddenly I thought, 'The cable has snapped!' I had always wondered how strong it was and now I was imagining the news headline: 'Twenty Tourists Go into Orbit in Pleasure Balloon.' The thought lasted only a split second as I quickly realized what had happened. The clouds had blown in from the sea, and the balloon was now in the middle of them. No doubt the bedraggled tourists were fervently wishing they could have their money back. The balloon was still there – it was just that there was something in the way.

God is still there, but we no longer enjoy the reality of his closeness or his love. We have cut ourselves off from him.

God may seem distant or even non-existent. However, that is not because he is, but rather because there is something in the way. Our rejection of him has separated us from him. We put ourselves, instead of him, at the centre of the universe. We can rebel against him, either by outright rejection or simply by ignoring him and living our own way. God is still there, but we no longer enjoy the reality of his closeness or his love. We have cut ourselves off from him.

Pain and death

Not only is human life difficult and often tough, but it is also painful and short. Pain itself can be a very useful thing. You just need to see the terrible effects of leprosy to realize just how bad it is not to be able to feel any pain. But now pain is taken to a new level. Human life begins with increased pain[8] and ends in death.[9] And sickness and death are alien invasions into God's good world.

Making sense of our world

This biblical account may seem very distant to us, but the kind of world it describes is very real. Why is it that we long for meaningful relationships and love, yet so often end up feeling alone? Why is it that every culture in the world has had some concept of the supernatural, and yet still God seems so far away? Why is the world sometimes a place of beautiful tranquillity and at other times a place of horrific destruction? Why do we love life and fear death?

We may reject the Genesis story as an antiquated myth but, if we stop long enough to think about it, it appears to make sense of our world in a way that nothing else does. Outside of the biblical account, we can often end up becoming either optimists who struggle to make sense of the bad stuff in our world or pessimists who are continually surprised by the good. I firmly believe that the Bible makes more sense of our experience of this world than any other philosophy or religion.

Compare the biblical concept with the view of the world presented by atheist Richard Dawkins:

> In a universe of blind physical forces and genetic replications some people are going to get hurt, some people are going to get lucky, and you won't find any rhyme or reason in it, nor any justice. The universe we observe has precisely the properties we should expect if there is at the bottom no design, no purpose, no evil and no good. Nothing but blind pitiless indifference. DNA neither knows nor cares. DNA just is and we dance to its music.[10]

But does the universe really look as if there is no evil and no good? I would suggest that our experience of life shows that there are things that are good and other things that are not. We long for intimacy and we fear rejection. We distinguish between that which is beautiful and what is not.

Evolution may try to explain these things. For instance, it may say that the reason why I long for relationships is that they are the best context in which to pass on my genes. But it would not explain why I might stay faithful to my wife, even if she was unable to have children. Richard Dawkins has to admit that this kind of behaviour does exist and he describes it as 'misfirings, Darwinian mistakes'. He goes on to call them 'blessed, precious mistakes',[11] but where he draws those values from is a mystery! Are our longings just a by-product of the evolutionary process and are some of our closest relationships simply Darwinian mistakes?

The Bible says no. Our feelings are connected to reality. The materialist who excludes God has to conclude that suffering, pain and death is just the way the world is. But the Bible says that, though this is the way the world is, it is not the way it should be, how it once was, nor how it one day will be. We hate death because it is bad. We long for love because that is what we were made for. We can distinguish between beauty and ugliness because there is some objective standard. This is, in many ways, good news. When we feel that there is something wrong with the world, it is not a cruel delusion or a pipe dream. There *is* something wrong with it. When we stand at the graveside of a friend and feel that it shouldn't be this way, we are right. It really shouldn't be this way.

In his book *Awakenings* (which later became a film by the same title), the neurologist Oliver Sacks explains:

> For all of us have a basic intuitive feeling that once we were
> whole and well; at ease, at peace, at home in the world;
> totally united with the grounds of our being; and that we lost
> this primal, happy, innocent state, and fell into our present
> sickness and suffering. We had something of infinite beauty and
> preciousness – and we lost it; we spend our lives searching for
> what we have lost; and one day, perhaps, we will suddenly
> find it . . .[12]

Reflecting on this, the Christian apologist Michael Ramsden said, 'How do you like that? How many dollars spent? How much research done? How many years invested, and we've finally got as far as Genesis chapter three!'[13]

Where can hope be found?

While it makes sense of our world, this chapter of the Bible is also pretty bleak. We want to live, but we will all die. We crave pleasure, but often experience pain. We long for relationships, yet can end up alone. We have a desire for the supernatural, but God seems distant and unknowable.

The artist Damien Hirst expressed it well: 'Why do I feel so important when I'm not? Nothing is important and everything is important. I do not know why I am here but I am glad that I am – I'd rather be here than not. I am going to die and I want to live forever. I can't escape that fact, and I can't let go of that desire.'[14]

Is there any hope that the world can change?

One of implications of the biblical teaching about sin is that we will have to reject superficial utopian ideas about the future. This is because the Bible shows that there is something radically wrong with the world that superficial solutions don't and won't address. The political philosopher and atheist John Gray explains the biblical teaching quite clearly:

> Human life is marked by human sin . . . Evil has been at work in
> every human heart since the Fall of Man; it cannot be defeated
> in this world. This doctrine gave Christianity an anti-utopian
> bent it never completely lost, and Christians were spared the
> disillusionment that comes to all who expect any basic change in
> human affairs. In Augustinian terms, the belief that evil can be
> destroyed, which inspired medieval millenarians and resurfaced
> in the Bush administration, is highly unorthodox.[15]

If there is to be genuine hope, we need a solution that really deals with the root causes of the human problem.

I spend quite a lot of my time in former communist countries. In theory, Marxism seemed a great idea to many people, but it failed to take seriously the human condition and therefore failed in practice. Gray correctly points out that orthodox Christianity will lead to a certain degree of pessimism about the world. The problems of our world are far deeper than we often imagine.

Hope, if genuine, is going to have to deal with the reality of evil.

Hope, if genuine, is going to have to deal with the reality of evil.

Gray's conclusion is that there is no hope. However, the biblical vision is different. And even in this bleak chapter of the Bible there is a seed of hope. We read that a descendant of the woman will crush the head of the snake and be responsible for the destruction of evil. The world we live in is not the way it once was, but neither is it the way it one day will be. The world was broken through the actions of a human being, but through another human being hope would come. He would give us a glimpse of what the world would one day be like.

3. BACK TO THE FUTURE I

God promised that one day his broken world would be put right. He would come back and sort it out. That promise is repeated and developed throughout the Old Testament part of the Bible. At times it seemed like real change would come, but raised hopes became shattered dreams, and by the end of the Old Testament things were looking as bleak as ever. Yet even then the promise came afresh from God in an even more vivid way. Take this example from the prophet Isaiah, writing in the eighth century BC:

In the last days

the mountain of the LORD's temple will be established
   as the highest of the mountains;
it will be exalted above the hills,
   and all nations will stream to it.

Many peoples will come and say,

'Come, let us go up to the mountain of the LORD . . .
   He will teach us his ways,
   so that we may walk in his paths.' . . .
He will judge between the nations
   and will settle disputes for many peoples.

They will beat their swords into ploughshares
   and their spears into pruning hooks.
Nation will not take up sword against nation,
   nor will they train for war any more.[1]

There is still hope that one day justice will be done and war will be no more. The prophet goes on to say,

The wolf will live with the lamb,
   the leopard will lie down with the goat,
the calf and the lion and the yearling together;
   and a little child will lead them.
The cow will feed with the bear,
   their young will lie down together,
   and the lion will eat straw like the ox.
The infant will play near the cobra's den,
   and the young child will put its hand into the viper's nest.
They will neither harm nor destroy
   on all my holy mountain,
for the earth will be filled with the knowledge of the LORD
   as the waters cover the sea.[2]

Even in the middle of bleak days, there was still hope that someone would come. One who would bring justice, destroying evil and helping the poor. But notice that this hope goes even further still. Even the natural order will be affected. The pictures are startling: a lion eating straw like an ox, a wolf sleeping next to a lamb, a child playing near previously deadly snakes. There will be nothing to cause harm. It's a wonderful and beautiful picture.

Yet at the time it seemed impossible. How would this hope ever be realized? For 400 years nothing had happened. Heaven had been silent. Things had carried on like normal. The promise seemed to have been forgotten.

Then one day a manual labourer from Nazareth turned up in the region of Galilee in northern Israel. He gathered a group of followers. They included a former tax collector, two hot-headed brothers, unschooled fishermen and a religious extremist. Not the most promising group to bring about world transformation. We pick up the story as this odd-bod group climb into a fishing boat one evening to make the seven-mile crossing to the other side of Lake Galilee.

Storm warning

That day when evening came, he said to his disciples, 'Let us go over to the other side.' Leaving the crowd behind, they took him along, just as he was, in the boat. There were also other boats with him. A furious squall came up, and the waves broke over the boat, so that it was nearly swamped. Jesus was in the stern, sleeping on a cushion. The disciples woke him and said to him, 'Teacher, don't you care if we drown?'

He got up, rebuked the wind and said to the waves, 'Quiet! Be still!' Then the wind died down and it was completely calm.

He said to his disciples, 'Why are you so afraid? Do you still have no faith?'

They were terrified and asked each other, 'Who is this? Even the wind and the waves obey him!'[3]

I have been to Lake Galilee several times and I can imagine nothing nicer after a hot busy day than a gentle sail at sunset. The sun was setting on the far shore, illuminating the surrounding hills in its warm evening light. The water was lapping softly against the side of the boat, and a gentle breeze was blowing those in it steadily towards their destination. After a busy day surrounded by crowds, this must have been a welcome break. At least that was how it all started.

Then things changed. The gentle breeze started to pick up and in no time at all it was battering the boat. Massive waves were swamping the little vessel. Now this kind of sudden change in the weather is not uncommon in that region. The unique setting of Galilee between the heights of Mount Hermon and the Dead Sea, the lowest point on earth, means that storms can blow through the lake with little or no warning. It appears though that this particular storm was uncommonly big. The disciples, some of whom were hardened fishermen, feared for their lives. Here was a storm of epic proportions.

Nature, which just a few moments before had seemed such an idyllic friend, was now a raging enemy. The wind that had been helping the occupants of the boat to their destination now threatened to destroy them. The water that had carried their boat was now on the verge of drowning them.

Not knowing what else to do, the disciples woke Jesus, who, remarkably, was sleeping through the whole event in the back of the boat. Exasperated by his apparent lack of concern for their predicament, they shouted, 'Teacher, don't you care if we drown?' I am not sure what they were expecting Jesus to do. If he was just a teacher, then he could possibly have given them a lesson in the climatic conditions leading to the storm! My guess is that they just wanted him to help bail the water out of the boat. But I doubt if anyone expected what happened next.

Jesus got up and rebuked the wind and the waves, in the same way that we might speak to a bunch of noisy children, telling them to 'shut up'! What is more remarkable is that they did. Not only did the wind stop, but it also was completely calm. The disciples, who moments before had feared for their lives, were now gripped with a new kind of fear. Who was this man who even nature obeyed?

I wonder if their fear arose not so much from the fact that they didn't know the answer to their own question, but rather that they thought they did? As the disciples were all Jews, they would have been familiar with the Old Testament part of the Bible. They would have known from the book of Psalms, written 1,000 years before, that the only person with power over the wind and the waves was God.[4] And yet here was a Galilean carpenter standing with them in a fishing boat doing exactly what God alone could do.

Do you really expect me to believe that?

Of course you may thinking right now, 'Nice story, but you don't actually expect me to believe that it happened, do you?' I agree that it is quite reasonable that we should come to such claims with a degree of scepticism. We would want very good reasons to believe them, not least because they are so very different from our own experience of life. Even as a Christian, open to the possibility of the miraculous, I still don't believe every reported miraculous event I hear about. My default position is one of scepticism, unless I am persuaded otherwise.

However, having said that, I am persuaded that there are good reasons to take seriously this account. For a start, there is strong evidence to show that the Gospel accounts

contain eyewitness evidence.[5] There are also simply too
many biblical manuscripts dating from too close to the date
of writing to argue that these stories were distorted or were
later additions.[6]

But did it actually happen? It is significant that this is
not the only such claim recorded in the Gospels. Jesus is
reported to have done many other similarly remarkable
things. While some of them were in front of relatively small
audiences, such as this one, others were very public and well
known. The very biggest claim of all is Jesus' own resurrection from the dead. Not only is it the most outrageous of
all the claims, but it is also the one that is most verifiable
(something we will examine later in chapter 7). So while I
can't give lots of external evidence for this event in particular, if the later and bigger miracles can be shown to be true,
then I don't have a problem accepting that this one could
also be true.[7]

Good party tricks?

So what if this did actually happen? What was Jesus' purpose
in doing such things? Calming storms, feeding thousands and
turning water into wine would be pretty good party pieces
with which to impress people and show them how great you
were. So are these miracles simply tricks to prove how great
Jesus really was?

It is certainly true that Jesus' miracles are powerful sign-
posts to who he is. Anyone could claim to be God, but it is
another thing altogether to do the kind of things that only
God can do. But the miracles are also much more than this.
Jesus is giving us glimpses of a future world. We get to see
his power over life's greatest enemies and his ability to bring
the change that we really need.

I love the *Back to the Future* trilogy of films. They humorously explore what could happen if you could travel through time. Yet what we have, especially in this and the following accounts in Mark's Gospel, is an opportunity really to go back to the future. Ironically, to see what the future looks like, we need to look back to the past. What we see in the miracles of Jesus are snapshots of what the future world will look like.

What we see in the miracles of Jesus are snapshots of what the future world will look like.

A glimpse of the future

As Jesus calms the storm, he is doing more than revealing who he is. He is showing that he is the one who can bring a chaotic creation under control. And this is good news to us because it was not just first-century fishermen who lived in fear of the power of nature.

Living in England as I do, it is sometimes hard to imagine being fearful of nature. It is never too hot or too cold. We don't get earthquakes worth reporting, and our only volcanoes are well and truly extinct. We don't fear storms and can even find them fun – a break from the mediocre weather that normally covers our land. Even our wildlife is pretty harmless – you would struggle to get killed by anything living on our shores. But that is certainly not the case for the majority of people in the world.

The morning of 26 December 2004 started like any other morning for thousands of holidaymakers enjoying the beaches of Thailand. Little did they know that the gentle waves lapping against the shore would soon be replaced by a gigantic 30-metre-high tsunami that would result in the deaths of over 230,000 people.

As I write this chapter I'm looking out over the idyllic Fish Hoek Bay in Cape Town on a beautiful summer's day. Visitors are enjoying the sandy beach and playing in the turquoise sea. Yet just a year ago, a fellow English tourist was attacked and killed by a shark in these same waters.

A friend of mine recently returned from doing medical work in Haiti. Long after the television news had stopped reporting on the events there, the country is still struggling to recover from the consequences of the magnitude 7.0 earthquake that killed over 100,000 people.

For a majority of the world's population, nature can be a real enemy. This can take many forms: earthquakes, volcanoes, tsunamis, hurricanes, fires, locusts, wild animals, cyclones, flooding and drought. All of these can bring devastation – some in just a matter of seconds.

Normally, after such disasters, some controversial church minister will hit the headlines by claiming that the event was a judgment from God, God's way of avenging the evil of that particular country. Yet we have no reason to suppose that this is the case. Jesus himself explained that the deaths of eighteen people in a natural disaster in Jerusalem were not because they were worse individuals than anyone else.[8] We should not presume that such disasters are specific judgments from God on a particular people, but reminders to all of us that we live in a broken world.

In the face of this natural power, we can feel helpless to do anything. We can try to limit the death toll, but our strategies are, at best, coping mechanisms. Who can control the power of a tsunami or change the path of a hurricane?

The staggering revelation, in this account, is that there is someone who has that kind of power. The one who calmed the storm has the power to control nature with just a word. What he did in the past he can and will do again.

One day Jesus will bring all of creation under his perfect control. No longer will people have to live in fear of the power of nature. Jesus didn't simply come to give people a spiritual experience or give me a connection with God. He came to mend a broken universe. As we have already seen, the biblical hope lies not in the destruction of this natural world, but in its transformation. For now it groans, broken and distorted, but one day it will be set free.

Imagine

In the shadow of Mount Gilboa in northern Israel lie the hot springs of Sachne. Natural volcanic springs feed a series of pools set among landscaped gardens, with water that is continually 28 °C. In the winter this can feel warm, but on a hot summer's day it is perfect for a cool and refreshing dip.

I remember swimming through these pools with a group of friends. We swam to the lowest pool where there were no other people, and then stopped for a second to take in our surroundings. The mountain slopes reached above us. Palm trees lined the banks and overhung the water. A gentle breeze rustled the leaves. The water was the perfect temperature – warm enough in which to feel comfortable but cool enough to be refreshing. Around us were all sorts of multicoloured fish gently tickling our feet as they swam past.

I stopped and thought. Even now we can catch a glimpse of what the world will one day be like. Or, as C. S. Lewis put it, these experiences are 'the scent of a flower we have not found, the echo of a tune we have not heard, news from a country we have never yet visited'.[9]

Our hope is that the one who stilled the storm will one day bring all of nature under his control. No longer will we fear nature as an enemy, but enjoy it as a friend. The moments when we enjoy this world best are just a foretaste of what is to come. A walk in the hills on a fresh spring day or an evening on the beach watching the sun slowly sink into the sea are just a glimmer of what is yet to come. Jesus has shown us a glimpse of what the world will one day be like.

But there is something even more unpredictable than the weather. It's the human heart. And what can Jesus do about that?

4. BACK TO THE FUTURE II

I will never forget my first experience of skiing. I had been invited by friends to join them on their family holiday in Colorado. They were all experienced skiers, and I was worried about embarrassing myself as a beginner. So before I left, I decided to get some lessons on my local dry slope.

After three hours of lessons, I figured I knew all I needed to know. I couldn't wait to be set free on real snow. Eventually the day came. We arrived at the slopes, I put on my skis and we headed for the chair lift. As we neared the top of the mountain, my pulse started to quicken. Miles of pristine snow lay in front of me. I was finally free to ski!

We unloaded at the top of the lift, and I slid slowly across the gentle slope where many others had stopped to do up their boots. I wasn't going very fast, but the slope was enough to keep me moving towards the edge of the first run. As I gradually picked up speed, I suddenly realized – I couldn't remember how to stop. Panic gripped me as I continued to gather speed down the slope. How could I stop? Then it hit me – the most stupid idea I have ever had. I figured the best way to stop was to ski into the trees! Off I slipped, over the edge of the piste and into the forest. In no time at all I was wrapped around a tree, both skis off, badly bruised and feeling very, very silly.

I soon discovered another way of stopping: falling over! This I managed to do several hundred times during the course of the day. My progress was so slow that I eventually had to be rescued and given a ride back to the bottom before it got dark!

I had thought that I was free to ski. But actually I was not free at all. It was only when I had properly learned to stop that I was really free to go. Freedom meant learning to control where I wanted to go, rather than being controlled by where the slope wanted me to go.

In the same way, we can feel that we are free in life. Free to do what we want. But it is often only when we try to stop that we realize we are not free at all, not in control of who we are or what we do.

This was certainly the case for the person Jesus met in his next encounter, immediately after the storm. As they landed on the far shore, he and his disciples probably felt in need of some sleep, but instead they were confronted with a scene more akin to a horror movie:

> They went across the lake to the region of the Gerasenes.
> When Jesus got out of the boat, a man with an impure spirit
> came from the tombs to meet him. This man lived in the
> tombs, and no one could bind him anymore, not even with
> a chain. For he had often been chained hand and foot, but he
> tore the chains apart and broke the irons on his feet. No one

was strong enough to subdue him. Night and day among the
tombs and in the hills he would cry out and cut himself with
stones.

When he saw Jesus from a distance, he ran and fell on his
knees in front of him. He shouted at the top of his voice,
'What do you want with me, Jesus, Son of the Most High
God? In God's name don't torture me!' For Jesus had said to
him, 'Come out of this man, you impure spirit!'

Then Jesus asked him, 'What is your name?'

'My name is Legion,' he replied, 'for we are many.' And he
begged Jesus again and again not to send them out of the area.

A large herd of pigs was feeding on the nearby hillside.
The demons begged Jesus, 'Send us among the pigs; allow us
to go into them.' He gave them permission, and the impure
spirits came out and went into the pigs. The herd, about two
thousand in number, rushed down the steep bank into the lake
and were drowned.

Those tending the pigs ran off and reported this in the
town and countryside, and the people went out to see what
had happened. When they came to Jesus, they saw the man
who had been possessed by the legion of demons, sitting
there, dressed and in his right mind; and they were afraid.
Those who had seen it told the people what had happened
to the demon-possessed man – and told about the pigs as
well. Then the people began to plead with Jesus to leave their
region.

As Jesus was getting into the boat, the man who had been
demon-possessed begged to go with him. Jesus did not let
him, but said, 'Go home to your own people and tell them
how much the Lord has done for you, and how he has had
mercy on you.' So the man went away and began to tell in
the Decapolis how much Jesus had done for him. And all the
people were amazed.[1]

Distant from our own experience?

At first, this account can appear very distant from our experience of life. Demon possession raises all kind of questions. Exactly what is it? Can it still happen today, and, if so, how? We may find it fascinating. In fact, it seems that there is often more intrigue about the devil than there is about God. But what does it all have to do with us?

It is worth knowing that the term for demon possession doesn't actually appear in the original language in which this book was written. It's a translation of just one word meaning literally 'demonized'. Rather than seeing it in black and white – some people being 'possessed' and others not – it seems to be more of a gradual thing. Evil and demonic power can increasingly take control of a person's life as they open themselves up to it. This man may seem totally different from anything in our experience, but a closer look reveals that he is not as different as we might at first think.

No control

The first thing we notice about this man is that his life is out of control. We don't know how things started out for him. But somehow his life has spiralled out of control. He can't control himself, and no-one else can control him, even though they have tried.

Far from others

I imagine that living in a graveyard had not always been this man's ambition. He's there because he can't live with other people. Cut off from his family and his community, he is lonely and isolated.

Far from God

Whenever we read of demon-possessed people meeting Jesus, their reaction is always the same: a disproportionate and irrational hatred. Clearly, they were unusually aware that, in the presence of Jesus, they were meeting more than just a man. Here was God himself.

Self-destructive

Not only was this man a danger to other people; he was also a danger to himself. His destructive behaviour has led him to cut himself with stones.

What about us?

In many ways, we are very different from this man. We don't run around naked in graveyards cutting ourselves with stones. But on reflection, are we really that dissimilar?

No control?

We like to think that we are in control of our lives. We make our own decisions and do whatever we want. While in some ways this is true, we can also be aware that it is not always the case. Sometimes we end up doing what we don't want to do or not doing what we really want to do. Often, as with my experience of skiing, it is only when we try to stop doing something that we realize how out of control we really are.

For those who don't believe this, here's a challenge. Try to live perfectly tomorrow. Try to always do and say the right thing. Try to be totally selfless and care only about what others think. When I've suggested this, people normally protest, 'But I don't want to.' However, the issue here is not whether we want to but whether we can. If we were totally free and in control, then we could. I guarantee to people that they will do well for a few hours. But then they will have to wake up to the truth!

It may be that you are only too aware of your own failures. You fail to live up to your own standards, let alone God's. Our problem is not that we don't know what we should do, but rather that we can't do it. I spoke to a student who admitted that he really respected and admired the Bible's teaching about sex. 'It's not that I don't think it's a good idea,' he admitted. 'It's just that I could never do it.' As G. K. Chesterton memorably put it, 'The Christian ideal has not been tried and found wanting. It has been found difficult; and left untried.'[2]

Far from others?

For many of us, the most important things in our lives are our relationships. Life's value is found not in how much we have or where we are, but who we are with. We want to love and be loved. So why is it then that we can end up cutting ourselves off from those we love the most? Why do we hurt those closest to us and risk ruining our relationships? How many times have we been left with regret because a relationship or friendship has broken down because of our own selfishness or mistakes? We can all too easily end up living in the lonely graveyard of broken relationships and regret.

Far from God?

I spend a lot of my life talking to people about Jesus. I'm often amazed at people's response to him. How can one person receive such love and worship, as well as such animosity and hatred? Why is Jesus' name worshipped by some but used as a swear word by others? Is it that, deep down, we sense that there is something more to him? If there is a God, and if Jesus is God, we can feel that we would rather he keep out of our lives and leave us alone.

Self-destructive?

One of the effects of our lack of control and broken relationships is that we can end up hating ourselves. For many, this is simply on the level of a dissatisfaction with who we are. But for some it is far more. Britain has one of the highest instances of self-harm in Europe.[3] Michelle is sixteen and she has had to deal not just with bullying at school, but also with her parents' broken marriage and a stepmother who hated her. She explains,

> A couple of years ago, I was changing for PE and noticed that one of my friends has bright red lines all the way down her arms; she usually wore long-sleeved tops, even in the summer, so I had never noticed them before. I was shocked, and she confided in me that she regularly cut herself. I couldn't understand why – she had everything, wealthy parents and wonderful holidays all over the world. She told me that her parents were never around and that she spent a lot of her time by herself. She felt that, when she cut herself, she got rid of the pain and the loneliness.
>
> I am now sixteen and have been regularly cutting myself for more than a year. I hide the knife or the scissors under the mattress and, when my mother goes to bed, I cut my arms and the top of my thighs. Some days are worse than others, particularly when I get upset.[4]

A story that at first seems totally disconnected from our lives turns out to be a lot more relevant than we had at first thought. Just as the man earlier was powerless to change himself or be changed by others, we can find that the same is true of us. We might want to change, but find that somehow we keep getting pulled down into the same self-destructive ways. The singer John Mayer expressed it well in his song 'Gravity'.[5] Despite finding his heart filled with love, he laments the fact that so often he throws it all away. Gravity keeps dragging him down. What is this force that keeps pulling us down, and is there any hope that things could ever change?

A friend of mine told me how, while she was studying at Harvard, she was in a psychology lecture with several psychiatrists. They discussed the problems of human nature. After some time, she tentatively asked what they thought the solution to the problem might be. They looked at her incredulously! The only solution they could offer was a diagnosis of the problem. They thought it was naïve to think there could actually be radical change in human nature.

As we look at human nature in general, and at our own lives in particular, we may ask ourselves whether real change is possible. Are we simply victims of our circumstances and genetics? Are our lives determined by forces outside of our control? Is there a possibility that we could change? Is there any hope for something better?'

Showdown

Into this man's desperate situation stepped Jesus. It was showdown time between good and evil. Between God and Satan. Some see good and evil as two equal and opposite forces to be kept in continual balance. The impression from this story is totally different. The result is not a hard-fought 0–0 draw. This is not Brazil versus Spain. This is Brazil taking on your local high-school team! There was never any question about who was going to win. Just as in the storm, Jesus' words were all that was needed to transform the situation. In a moment, the man was released from the demonic power controlling him, and a massive herd of pigs was drowned in the lake. Jesus did what no-one else can do. His authority over evil is clear.

> *Jesus did what no-one else can do. His authority over evil is clear.*

A comparison between the beginning and end of the story shows the dramatic transformation in this man's life.

No longer is he out of control, but dressed and in his right mind. No longer is he living in a graveyard, but he has been sent back home to his family. No longer does he hate Jesus, but he wants to follow him. No longer is he full of self-loathing, but he has dignity and respect.

This same Jesus can bring similar transformation today.

Mike was married with children and worked for his local newspaper. He can't pinpoint a time when he actually became an alcoholic. It all started with a few drinks after work, but after a while it was consuming his life, wasting his money and wrecking his marriage. He was forced to face reality when, for the second time, he was convicted for drink driving. He could easily have killed himself or someone else. Yet, even though he knew his life was a mess, he was powerless to change.

Things did change though. A young man turned up at work and he sat next to Mike. It turned out he was a Christian and would sometimes get into conversations with those around him. This annoyed Mike and he just told him to shut up! But one day they ended up talking alone. The colleague spoke to Mike about Jesus and his power to forgive and change people. Mike's response was to pray a simple prayer: 'Jesus, help!' It wasn't complicated but it was real. This was the moment that changed his life. Jesus did help. He not only cleaned up the past but gave Mike the power to change.

This story is not made up and neither is it unique. There are many stories that can be told of the transforming power of Jesus in people's lives today. They may not all sound so dramatic, but they are no less real.

There is of course a danger in presenting such stories. We can make it sound like, once a person has met Jesus, their life is simple from then on. Experience shows that this is not the case. Jesus can free us to be in control of our lives, but that doesn't mean we are free from the desires or temptation to do wrong things. Life is still a battle, even if it is one that can be won. Knowing Jesus can mend broken relationships, but those relationships can still have challenges. A relationship with God through Jesus is a wonderful thing, yet even though we can get to know him we still can't see him. It's like a long-distance relationship: there may be great communication, but it's still not as good as being together.

However, the difference that Jesus can make now is only the start of what he will actually do. What he does in part in the present, he will do fully and completely one day. The future hope that the Bible points to is the completion of the work that Jesus has started now. At the moment, we can enjoy a new relationship with God, but one day it will be so much better. Right now, we can enjoy relationships that are restored, but in the future they will be even more fulfilling. Today we can have the power to live differently, but one day we will be totally free.

Imagine

Imagine a world where we are not only truly free to do the right thing, but also free from the desire to do the wrong thing. This may sound boring, but the opposite is in fact the case. The new world that God will make is not like *Pleasantville* – the imaginary town from the film with the same name. The popular BBC TV programme *The One Show* ran a poll to discover Britain's 'favourite sins'. But sin is not the 'naughty-but-nice' stuff that makes life fun. Sin is the destructive stuff that wrecks our lives and relationships. One of the things I am looking forward to most about the new world is its freedom. Freedom from the temptation to do what I know is wrong. Freedom from doing what I know is painful to myself and others.

Imagine a world where relationships work the way they should. No bitterness, backbiting or gossip, hurtful words or selfish actions. People who continually look out for one another. Imagine having friends who think of how to serve one another and not themselves.

Imagine a world where you can relate to God as a close friend, not at a distance, but face to face. My brother's wife comes from Canada. For much of their engagement they lived 5,000 miles apart. Though they enjoyed being engaged it was nothing to the joy of finally being together. In the same way, the Bible describes our relationship to God now as the engagement – and the best is yet to come.

It may be that the idea of having a relationship with God doesn't excite you at all. Not now and not ever. But what kind of God are you imagining a relationship with? Many people's impression of God is 'a Stalin in the sky or a Hitler in the heavens'.[6] That kind of God exists to sap the life out of you and steal your joy. It's hardly surprising that you wouldn't want a relationship with a God like that. Christopher Hitchens famously described heaven as a 'celestial North Korea'.[7]

But the God we find in the Bible is so different. We have already thought about some of the gifts he has given us. The beauty of this world and the joy of loving relationships are gifts to us now, but there is so much more to come. The God

The God of the Bible comes not to take our life, but to give us life. Not to steal our joy, but to give us the deepest joy of all.

of the Bible comes not to take our life, but to give us life. Not to steal our joy, but to give us the deepest joy of all. He is a generous, sacrificial and loving God who is committed to your good. Wouldn't you want to know a God like that?

As we have gone back to the future, we have seen Jesus' power not only to control nature, but also to change the human heart. He can restore people's relationships to God and to others. He has given us a glimpse of what the world will one day be like. But what can he do about the biggest enemy of all: death?

5. BACK TO THE FUTURE III

There was a time when people didn't talk about sex. Today it is death that is not mentioned in polite conversation. It remains one of the last taboos of our culture. Part of the reason for this is that we don't know how to handle it. We have advanced in so many ways, but for death there seems to be no answer.

There are different ways in which we can try to cope with it. Some ignore it and pretend that it doesn't exist. In our culture this is easier than in others because we keep death at a distance. Yet even though we may try to not think about it, the reality is that we will all still face it.

Others deal with death by using humour. Woody Allen famously said, 'It's not that I'm afraid to die; I just don't want to be there when it happens.'[1] But for those facing the raw reality of bereavement, death is no laughing matter.

Another coping method is to sentimentalize. One children's book spoke about death in this way: 'The people you love don't really go away. They will always be there with you.' But that's rubbish. The whole problem is that they *do* go away. They are *not* always with you.

Facing up to death

For those who are willing to stop and think about it, death can be a scary thing. Perhaps that's why we don't like to think about it too much. Dealing with the death of her own mother, J. K. Rowling, author of the Harry Potter books, admitted,

> My books are largely about death . . . They open with the death of Harry's parents. There is Voldemort's obsession with conquering death and his quest for immortality at any price, the goal for anyone with magic . . . I so understand why Voldemort wants to conquer death. We're all frightened of it.[2]

Writing in the *Daily Telegraph*, Tom Chivers also expressed his fear of death:

> I'm terrified of death: my own, my loved ones', everyone's . . . the odds are good that, 100 years after my death, no-one will really know who I was . . . There will come a time when not only do you and I not exist, but no-one exists, no life exists . . . and all our loves, works and ambitions, quite literally might as well never have been. Which is pretty depressing . . . If you're an atheist, and this doesn't scare or depress you, then I admire and envy you. For me, it's an infinite tragedy.[3]

The singer, songwriter and political activist Annie Lennox put it this way: 'Death is death, and when you have a close-up, in-your-face experience of it you realise (unless you're terribly impervious) that, you know, this is just a temporary journey and you are not in the driving seat – or, if you are, you are not in full control.'[4] Bono says similarly, 'I haven't really accepted that there are some things that I can't control. I don't remember agreeing to people dying, people close to me, or even people I don't know – if they're dying for no reason – I can't accept that. I'm no good with death.'[5]

For all our advancements and discoveries, we still have nothing that deals with death. We stand powerless in the face of it. I remember the first time I was confronted by the reality of death as a child. My parents sat us down and explained that my sister's best friend from school had died. She had gone to sleep like normal the night before, but she never woke up. Even though I didn't know her very well, I remember the terrible realization that she was gone and would never come back. I was so used to 'grown-ups' being able to sort things out, but no-one could do anything about this. She was gone, and no-one could ever bring her back.

In the face of the reality of death, time can seem like an enemy. We are sometimes aware of just how fast our lives are passing by. We have moments of incredible joy, but they are tempered by the fact that we know they won't last. Perhaps you have had that experience while on holiday. You were in the middle of having an amazing time, free from the worries and cares of life as well as the depressing weather back home. But then you remembered – it wasn't going to last. That realization tainted the joy of the moment.

Yet it's not just holidays that come to an end. Everything will. No matter how fulfilled and satisfying our lives are, they too will end. Our closest relationships will one day be concluded either by our death or by others' deaths, and we are powerless to do anything about it.

This feeling of powerlessness in the face of death is nothing new, as this account from the Bible reveals:

When Jesus had again crossed over by boat to the other side
of the lake, a large crowd gathered around him while he was
by the lake. Then one of the synagogue leaders, named Jairus,
came, and when he saw Jesus, he fell at his feet. He pleaded
earnestly with him, 'My little daughter is dying. Please come
and put your hands on her so that she will be healed and live.'
So Jesus went with him.

A large crowd followed and pressed around him. And a
woman was there who had been subject to bleeding for twelve
years. She had suffered a great deal under the care of many
doctors and had spent all she had, yet instead of getting better she
grew worse. When she heard about Jesus, she came up behind
him in the crowd and touched his cloak, because she thought, 'If I
just touch his clothes, I will be healed.' Immediately her bleeding
stopped and she felt in her body that she was freed from her
suffering.

At once Jesus realized that power had gone out from him.
He turned around in the crowd and asked, 'Who touched my
clothes?'

'You see the people crowding against you,' his disciples
answered, 'and yet you can ask, "Who touched me?"'

But Jesus kept looking around to see who had done it. Then
the woman, knowing what had happened to her, came and fell
at his feet and, trembling with fear, told him the whole truth. He
said to her, 'Daughter, your faith has healed you. Go in peace and
be freed from your suffering.'

While Jesus was still speaking, some people came from the
house of Jairus, the synagogue leader. 'Your daughter is dead,'
they said. 'Why bother the teacher anymore?'

Overhearing what they said, Jesus told him, 'Don't be afraid;
just believe.'

He did not let anyone follow him except Peter, James and
John the brother of James. When they came to the home of the

synagogue leader, Jesus saw a commotion, with people crying and wailing loudly. He went in and said to them, 'Why all this commotion and wailing? The child is not dead but asleep.' But they laughed at him.

After he put them all out, he took the child's father and mother and the disciples who were with him, and went in where the child was. He took her by the hand and said to her, '*Talitha koum!*' (which means 'Little girl, I say to you, get up!').

Immediately the girl stood up and began to walk around (she was twelve years old). At this they were completely astonished. He gave strict orders not to let anyone know about this, and told them to give her something to eat.[6]

Desperation

Here were two people who were desperate.

Jairus's twelve-year-old daughter was sick. Jairus knew that she was dying and he was desperate for Jesus to help. No doubt he had heard about his miracles and longed for him to come. He didn't know where else to turn. His influential position in society and the wealth that came with it could not help his daughter's condition one iota. His hopes must have been raised when Jesus agreed to come. His main worry then was getting back to his house before it was too late. Crowds were in the way, and, frustratingly, Jesus didn't seem to be in the same hurry that he was in. You can imagine how agitated he must have got when all of a sudden Jesus stopped. He explained that someone had touched him. The comment confused everyone. There were loads of people touching him – he was after all in the middle of a crowd!

Trembling with fear, another desperate individual came and fell at Jesus' feet, just as Jairus had done a few moments before. This woman had been sick for as long as Jairus's daughter had been alive. She had spent all her money on doctors but, instead of growing better, she had simply got worse. Not knowing where else to turn, she thought that, if she could only touch Jesus' clothes, she could be healed. What no doctor could do in twelve years, Jesus was able to do in an instant. The woman left, free from suffering and at peace.

Yet all the time, Jairus must have been thinking about his daughter. Couldn't Jesus hurry up? Why did he have to stop? If the woman had already been healed, then why hold a conversation about it? And then he spotted his servants: the look on their faces said it all. It was over. His daughter was dead. The bottom fell out of Jairus's world. What good was it now? While she was alive there had been a chance that Jesus could heal her, but now? It was too late.

Jesus' response was to turn to Jairus and tell him, 'Don't be afraid; just believe.' If that was surprising, then his next words were even more incredible. On reaching the house, he was confronted with the professional mourners who would have been hired for such occasions. He told them to get out of the house, explaining that the child was 'not dead but asleep'. They knew the difference between death and sleep and they thought that Jesus was crazy.

Once they had all left and the house had grown quiet, Jesus took the little girl by the hand and simply told her to get up – and she did. Just as we might wake a sleeping person, Jesus raised the dead. No wonder all those who witnessed it were astonished. Who was this who could not only heal the sick but also raise the dead?

Nice story, but what about us?

So what does this story mean for us today? Do those who follow Jesus never get sick and die? Does Jesus promise always to heal those who have enough faith? There are certainly many accounts of Jesus' power to heal today. But even if these were all authentic, there are certainly plenty of people who *don't* get healed now. Even in the Bible, some of the early Christian leaders who healed others had sicknesses from which they never received healing. And while Jesus had the power to raise the dead, we only read of him using it three times. Today many Christians will suffer in different ways. And even those who do experience some kind of healing will one day die of something or other.

This account above is not an assurance that following Jesus will mean a life free from pain. What we see here is another glimpse of the future in the past. Here is a hint of what God's new world will be like. A world without sickness and death. In the penultimate chapter of the Bible we catch another glimpse of what that world will be like: "'He will wipe every tear from their eyes. There will be no more death" or mourning or crying or pain, for the old order of things has passed away.'[7] Here is a world without hospitals, hankies or hearses. Here is the world as we want it to be. Here is a world where the good things never have to come to an end.

Here is a world without hospitals, hankies or hearses. Here is the world as we want it to be.

Towards the end of *The Lord of the Rings*, Samwise Gamgee meets a friend who he thought was dead. He exclaims, 'Gandalf! I thought you were dead! But then I thought I was dead myself. Is everything sad going to come untrue? What's happened to the world?'[8]

In Genesis chapter 3 we saw a world that was broken. People's relationships with one another and with God had been damaged. Sickness and death had invaded God's good world. But here in Mark's Gospel we have seen Jesus' power to make the sad things 'untrue'.

The disciples were powerless to do anything about the storm. The people in the town were powerless to control the demon-possessed man. The doctors were powerless to help the sick woman, and Jairus was powerless to save his daughter. But with a word, Jesus could still the storm and set the man free. With just a touch, he could heal the sick and raise the dead.

Two thousand years have passed, but we are still faced with the same enemies. We may be more advanced in many ways. Yet we still lack the power really to change nature, the human heart or death. Jesus is just as relevant to us today as he ever was. He can do what no-one else can.

Imagine

We've seen three snapshots of what the world will one day be like. These are only a glimpse but they may help us to start to imagine it for ourselves. John Lennon encouraged people to imagine that there was no heaven.[9] Well, don't imagine heaven – imagine this world as it will be like, one day.

Think of the most beautiful place you have ever been to. Perhaps a secluded and sandy cove next to a turquoise ocean, on a summer's day. Or maybe a lush green valley winding through snow-capped mountains. Remember what it was like – the smell of the air, the feel of the warm breeze on your skin, the majestic beauty of nature taking your breath away.

Then remember, if you can, one of the best times you have ever had with your friends. A time when you enjoyed one another's company so much that you almost forgot yourself. A time when you felt completely loved, secure and accepted.

Now think of what it could be like to know God. Not as a distant deity, but as a friend who is by your side. A God who is not only totally powerful, but utterly loving and completely committed to your good.

Finally, remember a time, if there was one, when you were totally fit and healthy. Think of a period in your life when you were free from pain, sickness and tiredness. Maybe there has never been a time like that for you. If not, then imagine what it would be like to have a body that works the way it should: to be free to run and dance without ever becoming tired or weary.

Then take all of those thoughts: the breathtaking beauty of nature; the love and security of friends; the knowledge that God was close and real and for you; and the healthy body free from pain and sickness. Add all of them together. Multiply that enjoyment by a million. Then take away the fear that they would ever have to come to an end.

Doesn't it feel good?

You are just starting to glimpse what God's new world could be like.

6. ALL HELL BREAKS LOOSE

As we have travelled 'back to the future', we have been able to catch a glimpse of what the world will one day be like: a creation set free, relationships restored, and all to be enjoyed with new bodies, free from sickness and death. We've been able to start to imagine and even taste what it might all be like. Our deepest joys now are just a shadow of what is yet to come. In C. S. Lewis's *The Last Battle*, one of the animals explains its joy at finally arriving in the new Narnia: 'I've come home at last! This is my real country! I belong here. This is the land I have been looking for all my life, though I never knew it till now. The reason why we loved the old Narnia is that sometimes it looked a little like this.'[1]

We have seen something of the astounding hope of a world made new. But we can't avoid the fact that the Bible also speaks about another reality in the future. What about hell? We may not like to speak of it, but we can't avoid the subject. Hell is not simply the invention of medieval artists and theologians. Jesus himself spoke about a day and a place of judgment. What is hell really like?

In many ways, hell is the opposite of the new world that God will make. Hell is a place of chaos, fear and destruction, a place of selfishness and broken relationships. Hell is separation from God and from his love. Hell is described as a place of pain and death. Of course, some of the Bible's descriptions of hell may be metaphorical, but if they are, then they are metaphors for a place that we wouldn't ever want to go to. Ever.

We sometimes speak of our experiences as being heavenly or hellish. This is often closer to the truth than we might imagine. Because the Bible emphasizes the continuity between this current age and the age to come, our experiences now are often a foretaste of the future.

Heavenly and hellish

We have already seen that we can catch a glimpse of God's new world in the beauty of nature or through the love of friends. But it is also true that, in our lives now, we can sometimes see the ugliness of hell. We see it when we watch the fear, death and destruction of an earthquake or tsunami. We feel it when we experience the heart-wrenching pain of broken relationships and shattered promises. We understand it when God seems distant and uncaring. We experience it when we go through the pain of sickness or the grief of losing a loved one. We can rightly describe these experiences as hellish, for that is what they are. One teenager summed it up when he said, 'Hell is like the feeling I had when my parents got divorced, but it will go on forever.'

While the idea of judgment and hell can seem wholly negative to us, this is not necessarily the case. The Bible affirms that ultimately there will be a day of justice. Deep down, we long for justice to be done and we are angered when it isn't – even in trivial matters like sport.

I remember watching England play Germany in the World Cup. Despite clearly crossing the line by a good metre, the English goal wasn't allowed – and several years later I am still bitter! How much more serious though are the injustices of real life? How often do people literally get away with murder? And even when criminals are brought to account, what kind of justice can there be to compensate for some of the horrors that we have witnessed on our planet?

The fact that there is a day of judgment is good news. Those who have escaped justice all their lives will one day be brought to account. The opposite would be a God who didn't care and turned a blind eye to the evils of this world. God *does* care and he wants justice to be done.

But what about me?

Where does this leave me? I may not be as bad as I could be, but am I as good as I should be? We like to simplify things by talking of the evil people 'out there', but what about the evil we find in our own hearts?

The Bible teaches that what makes our wrongdoing most serious is not simply *what* we do, but the one against whom we do it. Our actions are expressions of our self-declared independence from God. We may not always deny his existence, but we can live as if he didn't really matter. Ultimately, God gives people what they choose. If we want God to leave us alone to live as we please, then he will. He gives us the dignity of that choice.

I sometimes meet people who glibly say that that they would like to go to hell. After all, they say, that is where their friends will be. But hell is no party, and there is no friendship

> *Hell is not just separation from God but also from all of his good gifts.*

in hell. Hell is not just separation from God but also from all of his good gifts.

I remember when I moved away from home for the first time. On the first night I kicked my clothes into the corner of the room, like I had always done at home, and got into bed, delighted that I was finally free. I was independent and I could do whatever I wanted. After several days a few things started to happen. The first was that a large pile of dirty clothes had built up in the corner of my room. This had never happened before. Somehow they had always come back washed and ironed, with no effort on my part at all. The second thing was that the en-suite bathroom got increasingly dirty, to the point where it was actually quite unpleasant to use. In the past the bathroom had always been clean. What was happening? Well, of course, I was discovering that independence from my parents meant that many of the things I had taken for granted for so long were no longer there. I wasn't sure if I had ever said thank you to my mum for cleaning the bathroom or doing the laundry, which she had done every week of my life without fail.

More seriously, we may not have had much time for God in our lives up till now, but all of us experience and enjoy his many gifts, even if we never stop to say thank you. He gives us gifts like friendship, food and fun; skiing, sunshine and sex; holidays, homes and happiness. Yet so often we take the gifts and ignore the giver. If we choose to live without God in this life, then he will allow us to live without him in the future. Yet all the things that we take for granted now will not be there.

The reality is that, in different ways, all of us have gone

our own way. None of us is the person we should be. No-one ever was. No-one ever will be.

Except one.

Looking at the life of Jesus, I am struck not only by his power but also by his humanity and his compassion. He loves the outcast. He cares for the downtrodden. He has time for individuals and cares for their needs. He doesn't repay evil for evil, and yet he is not weak. He rebukes hypocrisy, particularly in the religious leaders of his day, and he challenges the status quo.

As I look at the life of Jesus, I can't help but think to myself: What would the world be like if everyone lived like him? In Jesus we don't just find true deity, but also true humanity: life as it was meant to be lived. Yet the biggest shock comes at the close of his life. After selflessly helping, serving and loving others, he ends up being executed. Why?

The crucifixion

Then the governor's soldiers took Jesus into the Praetorium and gathered the whole company of soldiers around him. They stripped him and put a scarlet robe on him, and then twisted together a crown of thorns and set it on his head . . . Then they led him away to crucify him . . .

Those who passed by hurled insults at him, shaking their heads and saying, 'You who are going to destroy the temple and build it in three days, save yourself! Come down from the cross, if you are the Son of God!' In the same way the chief priests, the teachers of the law and the elders mocked him. 'He saved others,' they said, 'but he can't save himself! He's the king of Israel! Let him come down now from the cross, and we will believe in him.' . . . In the same way the rebels who were crucified with him also heaped insults on him.

From noon until three in the afternoon darkness came over all the land. About three in the afternoon Jesus cried out in a loud voice, *'Eli, Eli, lema sabachthani?'* (which means 'My God, my God, why have you forsaken me?') . . .

And when Jesus had cried out again in a loud voice, he gave up his spirit.

At that moment the curtain of the temple was torn in two from top to bottom . . .

When the centurion and those with him who were guarding Jesus saw the earthquake and all that had happened, they were terrified, and exclaimed, 'Surely he was the Son of God!'[2]

Did you notice what is happening?

A broken relationship with his environment

Back in the third chapter of the first book of the Bible we are told that thorns and thistles were one of the evidences of the fact that we live in a broken world. Now these thorns were made into a crown that was ruthlessly and painfully pushed down upon Jesus' head. Jesus was literally bearing one of the very signs of our broken world. Not only that, but as Jesus hung on the cross the sky went black for three hours. At the point when the sun should have been at its brightest, darkness fell. Then, when Jesus finally breathed his last, there was an earthquake that terrified those who were witnessing the crucifixion events. It seemed as if creation itself was coming undone.

A broken relationship with others

Jesus had spent his life serving, helping and healing others. Yet here, at the moment when he needed them the most, his followers deserted him. One of his followers even betrayed

him for money. The crowds who had enthusiastically wel-
comed him now called for his death. He was the focus of
hatred, scorn and ridicule. The religious leaders, the Roman
soldiers, the crowds, and even those dying alongside him,
heaped abuse on him both verbally and physically.

A broken relationship with God

Yet there is a greater pain that Jesus experiences, even
worse than abandonment by his followers and friends. More
painful than the physical torture of crucifixion, Jesus now
faces separation from his own Father. In every other instance
Jesus has always addressed God as his Father. But now he
cries out in far more distant terms, 'My God, my God, why
have you forsaken me?'

The pain of a broken relationship is directly proportional
to the length of time that two people have been together
and the depth of love that existed between them. That is
why the death of a spouse is so incredibly more painful than
breaking up with someone with whom you've only had one
date. Imagine the pain that Jesus felt. For all eternity he had
enjoyed infinite yet intimate love from his Father. Here on
the cross that relationship is broken, and Jesus experiences
the agony of the separation.

Pain and death

None of the Gospel writers went into much detail about the
physical pain of crucifixion. They didn't need to. Anyone
living in the first-century Roman Empire was only too aware
of its horror. Such was its barbarity that the word was not
even mentioned in polite company. Two thousand years
later and our language still resonates with the pain: the word
'excruciating', for example, is derived from the word 'crucifixion'. When Mel Gibson's film *The Passion of the Christ* was

released, many complained that its violence was gratuitous. Yet whether or not it was right to depict it, the film simply portrayed what is likely to have happened.

A living hell

What is happening as Jesus dies? He is experiencing the very opposite of what the world should and will be like. He is literally experiencing hell. One famous Christian creed talks about Jesus descending to hell. But the hell that Jesus experienced was not after, but before, his death.

Jesus is the one person who didn't deserve to experience any of it. Yet he takes all hell on the cross. The staggering thing is that, as we read through the Gospels, we see that this is no sad accident. Nor is it the unfortunate end to a promising career. This was why he came. This was always the plan. Jesus knew he was going to die. He walked into Jerusalem knowing what was going to face him, and he still did it. Why?

One of the things that Jesus is mocked for on the cross is that he could save others but he couldn't save himself. That statement is incredibly ironic. Jesus knew that the only way ultimately to save others was by *not* saving himself. The hell that Jesus experienced on the cross was not what he deserved, but it was what *we* deserved. He was taking our place.

Some people have found the concept of Jesus dying in our place on the cross offensive. How could God punish an innocent man to get us off the hook? But elsewhere in the Bible it says that, on the cross, 'God was in Christ, reconciling the world to Himself'.[3] The one dying on the cross was not a third party that God had unfairly picked on. God was taking upon himself the cost and pain of our forgiveness and reconciliation.

What does this mean for us?

What does this mean for us? Firstly, this means that hell is really serious. If it was not, then why would Jesus have gone to such lengths to save us from it? Yet the only way to hell is literally over Jesus' dead body. He has done everything possible so that we wouldn't have to go there. There is nothing more that he can do than what he has already done.

Secondly, the cross shows us how thankful we should be. Imagine that a student comes home from a day at university. His housemate tells him that, while he was out, someone came round to collect a debt of his that had been outstanding. But the housemate goes on to explain that he had decided to pay on his behalf, and so the student doesn't need to worry about it any more. How thankful should the student feel? Well, it depends how big the debt was in the first place. If it had been merely a few pence postage for a letter, then a simple 'thank you' would be enough. But what if his housemate had just paid off his entire overdraft? He would be amazed. In the same way, when we understand quite how much Jesus paid for us, we realize how thankful we should be. Jesus experienced hell on the cross. He took it upon himself so that we don't have to.

Finally, the death of Jesus shows us that God's new world is not a reward to be earned. Rather, it is a gift to be received. If we could earn our way, then Jesus' death was unnecessary. God himself has paid the cost and done everything. We don't need to add to this. Anyway, we can't.

One of the best illustrations of this comes from Luke's account of the crucifixion. Matthew has already told us that there were two criminals crucified on either side of Jesus. Both of them started out cursing and mocking Jesus, along with everyone else. However, Luke records that something

happened to one of the criminals while he was hanging on
the cross. He stopped insulting Jesus and actually challenged
the other thief to do the same: 'We are punished justly, for
we are getting what our deeds deserve. But this man has
done nothing wrong.'⁴ At some point during the last few
hours the man had realized there was something different
about Jesus. Jesus didn't curse like everyone else, but rather
forgave the very people who were crucifying him.

He then turned to Jesus and said, 'Remember me when
you come into your kingdom.'⁵ This is a remarkable thing
to ask a naked man who is being crucified and is about to
die. Yet this criminal had realized something that others
had failed to see. Jesus' death was not spelling the end of
his promise to bring about a new kingdom. Neither had his
death ruined God's plan to change the world. Rather, it was
the very means by which it would happen.

Jesus' response to this man was equally astounding. He
turned to the man and said, 'Truly I tell you, today you will
be with me in paradise.'⁶ Here is a man who has led such a
bad life that he has ended up being crucified for his actions.
Yet Jesus is able to assure him that everything is going to be
OK. How could Jesus promise paradise to such a man, a man
who had no opportunity to make up for his bad actions? He
can't put right what he did wrong. Nor can he hop off the
cross and go to church, be baptized, read the Bible or help
old ladies across the road.

Jesus was able to offer such hope because he had taken
upon himself what this man deserved. He had taken upon
himself what we all deserve so that we can have what we
don't deserve. In the same way, we don't need to do anything to earn his forgiveness, nor can we. Simply recognizing
who Jesus is and trusting him is all we need.

Jesus not only gives us a glimpse of what the world will

one day be like, but it is because of what he has done that we
can be a part of it. Yet how can we know for sure that what
he died to accomplish really was accomplished? How do we
know that Jesus' death wasn't in fact the end?

7. WISHFUL THINKING?

I'm a pessimist by nature. I have always remembered the advice given to me as a child when I was excited about the possibility of winning a competition. 'Always expect the worst,' I was told. 'Then you won't be disappointed if it doesn't happen, and you'll be pleasantly surprised if it does.'

Such a view can protect us from disappointment, but it can also rob us of the joy of anticipation. Yet for those who have been let down by broken promises and disappointed by hopes that did not materialize, such a view is understandable. How do we know that Jesus really can deliver on his promise for a new world? How can we know that this isn't the cruellest delusion of them all?

You can't is the answer that John Gray gives in his book *Black Mass*. In it, the atheist philosopher discusses the hope that Jesus claimed to offer the world:

The teaching of Jesus was that the old world was about to come
to an end and a new kingdom established. There would be
unlimited abundance in the fruits of the earth. Those who dwell
in the new kingdom – including the righteous dead, who will
be raised back to life – would be rid of physical and mental ills.
Living in a new world that is without corruption, they will be
immortal. Jesus was sent to announce this new kingdom and rule
over it. There is much that is original and striking in Jesus' ethical
teaching. He not only defended the weak and powerless as other
Jewish prophets had done, but he also opened his arms to the
outcasts of the world. Yet the belief that a new kingdom was at
hand was the heart of his message and was accepted as such by
his disciples.

The only problem, Gray says, is that it didn't happen. He
explains, 'The new kingdom did not arrive, and Jesus was
arrested and executed by the Romans.' He quotes Albert
Schweitzer who captured this predicament when he wrote,

> In the knowledge that he is the coming son of man, Jesus lays
> hold of the wheel of the world to set it moving on that last
> revolution that is to bring all ordinary history to a close. It refuses
> to turn and he throws himself upon it. When it does turn it
> crushes him.[1]

For the early followers of Jesus, as for John Gray, the crucifixion seemed like the end of the story. Two of them
were walking from Jerusalem to a nearby village just three
days after the crucifixion. They were met by someone who
appeared to be a stranger. He asked them what they were
talking about and why they looked so depressed. They were
astonished that he didn't seem to know what had just happened in the city. One of them enquired, 'Are you the only

one visiting Jerusalem who does not know the things that have happened there in these days?'

'What things?' he asked.

'About Jesus of Nazareth,' they replied. 'He was a prophet, powerful in word and deed before God and all the people. The chief priests and our rulers handed him over to be sentenced to death, and they crucified him; but we had hoped that he was the one who was going to redeem Israel.'[2]

They thought that Jesus' death was also the death of their hopes. But everything would change when they realized that the one they were talking to was in fact Jesus himself, risen from the dead.

The foundation of hope

The death of Jesus, on its own, would have been the death of hope. But together with the resurrection, it can be the very basis of it. That is why, whenever early Christian leaders explained what they believed, they always mentioned *both* the crucifixion and the resurrection of Jesus. The crucifixion alone would be insufficient. One of those leaders, called Paul, put it this way:

But if it is preached that Christ has been raised from the dead, how can some of you say that there is no resurrection of the dead? If there is no resurrection of the dead, then not even Christ has been raised. And if Christ has not been raised, our preaching is useless and so is your faith. More than that, we are then found to be false witnesses about God, for we have testified about God that he raised Christ from the dead. But he did not raise him if in fact the dead are not raised. For if the dead are not raised, then Christ has not been raised either. And

if Christ has not been raised, your faith is futile; you are still in
your sins. Then those also who have fallen asleep in Christ are
lost. If only for this life we have hope in Christ, we are of all
people most to be pitied.[3]

Paul links the future hope of resurrection and the defeat of
death with the resurrection of Jesus in the past. They go
together. No resurrection means no hope. But if Jesus was
raised, then he is the prototype of what can one day happen to
us. Just as Jesus went through death and received a new body
never to die again, so we can too, if we trust him. Our future
hope is linked to the past event. This means that Christian hope
is not based on wishful thinking about the future, but an objective understanding about what happened in history.

Christian hope is not based on wishful thinking about the future, but an objective understanding about what happened in history.

I'm writing this book just a few miles from the southern
tip of Africa. Before the end of the fifteenth century, no
European sailor had ever successfully navigated beyond
this point. The treacherous seas at the meeting point of the
Atlantic and Indian oceans made it highly dangerous. Some
had tried and failed, and so the headland was known as 'the
Cape of Storms'. Then in 1497, the Portuguese sailor Vasco
da Gama did what others had failed to do. He not only made
it past the Cape, but all the way to India and back again. After
this, the point was given a new name: the Cape of Good
Hope.

This is a great illustration of death. How do we know what
lies beyond it? Are wishful thinking and mere speculation all

we have to go on? How can we know what is round the headland, when all of us stand on the same side of it and will one day be dashed against its rocks? But Jesus' resurrection means that he has not only sailed through death, defeating its power, but he has also come back. As a result, he can tell us that, rather than being a place of storms and fear, it can be a place of hope.

However, the biggest question remains.

How do we know that it really happened?

I remember speaking with a medical doctor about the resurrection. She looked at me in astonishment when I explained that I believed it was an actual historical event. She explained that she could not accept it because it was medically impossible. On another occasion a student commented, 'I could never believe in the resurrection of Jesus because that kind of thing doesn't happen every day.'

My response was, 'Exactly! It doesn't happen every day, and that is precisely why we should investigate it.'

Another student said to me, 'I'd only believe in the resurrection if we had lots of examples of it happening today.'

'But if it happened all the time,' I replied, 'then we wouldn't even be thinking about Jesus' resurrection – it wouldn't be any big deal.'

On one level, the claim of the resurrection is outrageous. It is unique in all of history. We won't and shouldn't expect to find a repeat of it. It is therefore all the more astonishing that people should believe it. But it is not just simple, naïve and uneducated people who buy it. There are intelligent, rational and well-respected scholars who also believe in the historicity of this event. How could these people be persuaded to believe in such a claim?

The answer lies in the fact that, though the resurrection

may be medically unrepeatable, statistically unlikely and philosophically impossible (at least according to our current worldview), there is in fact a great weight of historical evidence pointing towards it. In fact, so strong is the historical case that it has often persuaded those who would otherwise be very unlikely to accept it. One such individual was Pinchas Lapide, an Orthodox Jew, who, after studying the evidence, had to admit that he believed in the resurrection of Jesus of Nazareth.[4]

In my experience, those who ridicule the resurrection most are also those who have never really looked at the historical evidence. In a recorded discussion with the Christian professor John Lennox,[5] Richard Dawkins mocks the idea of the physical resurrection of Jesus and claims never to have met a respected Christian who seriously believed it. But what is more surprising is that it also seems that Dawkins was unfamiliar with some of the basic evidence for it.

Looking at the evidence

So what is the evidence? The philosopher William Lane Craig explains,

> We may be surprised to learn that the majority of New
> Testament critics investigating the gospels . . . accept the central
> facts undergirding the resurrection of Jesus. I want to emphasize
> that I am not talking about evangelical or conservative scholars
> only, but about the broad spectrum of New Testament
> critics who teach at secular universities and non-evangelical
> seminaries. Amazing as it may seem, most of them have
> come to regard as historical the basic facts which support the
> resurrection of Jesus.[6]

So what do we know about the events surrounding the claim of Jesus' resurrection, and what is it that scholars generally agree upon?

Jesus died

Firstly, we know that Jesus was crucified. This is supported both from within the Bible and in other Jewish and Roman sources. The Romans were very good at executing people. There is only one account of someone surviving crucifixion. It occurred when Josephus saw three of his friends being crucified. He pleaded with Titus, the soon-to-become emperor, for their lives, and Titus allowed for them to be taken down. In spite of this, two of them still died from their wounds.

We also have several other pieces of evidence that show that Jesus was dead. The soldiers did not bother to break his legs (to speed his death), for they already saw that he was dead. To verify this, they plunged a spear into his heart. Out came blood and water: medical confirmation of his death.

The soldiers carrying out such executions also had a vested interest in doing it well. If they didn't, their own lives would probably be demanded instead.

Jesus was buried

Not only was Jesus crucified, but it is well established that he was buried in the tomb belonging to a man called Joseph of Arimathea. What makes Joseph interesting is that he was one of the Jewish ruling council that had condemned Jesus to death. The fact that Joseph volunteered to allow his tomb to be used for a proper burial would seem a strange detail to include, if it were not in fact true. It would appear therefore that the whereabouts of Jesus' body would have been well known to people in Jerusalem. No other competing burial accounts exist.

The tomb was empty

Three days after the crucifixion, the tomb was reported to be empty by a group of women. Again, this would be an even stranger detail to make up, if the account were indeed fictitious. In first-century Roman society, the testimony of a woman was considered worthless in a court of law. If you were producing a fabricated story, why would you choose the first witnesses of the biggest event of all to be those who would have been regarded as unreliable? There appears to be no reason why this detail would have been recorded, if in fact it were not the case.

Even the Jewish scholar Geza Vermes concluded that the tomb must have been empty. He states, 'In the end when every argument has been considered and weighed, the only conclusion acceptable to the historian must be . . . that the women who set out to pay their last respects to Jesus found to their consternation, not a body, but an empty tomb.'[7]

There is also another piece of fascinating evidence that seems to support the empty tomb: an inscription of an edict from the Roman emperor that dates from around the time, discovered in the town of Nazareth. It warns against meddling with tombs and demands capital punishment for any such offender – an unusually serious penalty for such a crime. In all likelihood, the Roman governor Pilate would have had to file a report explaining that something had happened to the tomb, and this was quite possibly the official reaction.

People claimed to have met the risen Jesus

Many individuals claimed that they had seen Jesus after the resurrection. This happened to different people and in various ways and at different times. Sometimes to individuals and other times to crowds – once to as many as 500, all at the same time. Some may say that these people were simply hallucinating. However, this reasoning is inadequate. Hallucinations are experienced by individuals, but not by crowds of people simultaneously. They normally happen to certain types of people, but the resurrection appearances were to many different individuals. Hallucinations normally continue over a long period of time, but all the appearances of Jesus stopped suddenly, six weeks after the resurrection.

Nor is it likely that these people would have made the story up. So convinced were they by what they had seen that they held on to their conviction, even though for many it meant opposition and persecution and death. People may die for things that are not true, but why would someone die for something they *know* is not true?

The growth of the church

Finally, we have the existence of the church up till today. The biggest sociological phenomenon in history was founded on the belief that Jesus rose from the dead. The two most basic practices of the church – baptism and the Lord's Supper (eating bread and drinking wine in remembrance of Jesus) – had at their heart the belief in the resurrection. Baptism was a picture of resurrection to new life, and the belief was that the risen Jesus was present with his people as they commemorated his death. The day of rest also changed (not an easy thing to arrange in any culture!) from Saturday to Sunday to commemorate the day of resurrection.

What is more, the church grew and became established, not decades later in a different country, but in the very city and in the same generation in which these events are recorded to have taken place. Why did so many believe it? If Christianity was based on a fabrication, then why were the authorities, desperate as they were to suppress Christianity, so powerless to stop its spread? The evidence would have been right at their fingertips.

A resurrection-sized hole in history

None of the individual evidences alone will necessarily convince you, but, taken together, we see a 'resurrection-sized hole' in history that only the resurrection will truly fit. That is not to say that every scholar who accepts the claims I have made also believes in the resurrection. But I'm convinced that, once we have examined the evidence, the alternative explanations end up being even more incredible than the original proposition – that Jesus really did rise from the dead.

A look at the alternatives

Each generation seems to present a new alternative for what could have happened. The problem is that, because none of these alternatives has sufficient explanatory power to deal with all the evidence, none of them actually sticks. Here are a few that have been suggested:

Jesus didn't really die

As we have already seen, the Roman soldiers responsible for the crucifixion of Jesus had a vested interest in doing their job well. If they didn't, then their lives were at stake. The evidence that Jesus was in fact dead is convincing. Yet even if somehow he was not, we are still expected to believe another remarkable series of occurrences. Firstly, Jesus would have had to unwrap himself from a mass of burial clothes before rolling away the stone that covered the tomb, and then beat it past a Roman guard. Then he would have had to convince his disciples that he wasn't in fact a very sick man in need of emergency medical treatment, but the living God who had just conquered death! Anyone suffering what Jesus had been through would have been unable to walk, let alone pull off a con-trick of that magnitude.

The women went to the wrong tomb

Perhaps, in the darkness of the early morning, the women took a wrong turning and, without the help of a smart phone with GPS, ended up at another tomb?

But was this really likely? We are told that they had seen where Jesus was laid, and anyone who has buried a loved one knows only too well that you don't quickly forget the location. Are we to suppose that the other disciples who later came to inspect the tomb also went to the wrong one, including Joseph who actually *owned* the tomb? What's more, the tomb was not technically empty – it still contained the burial clothes.

Had it somehow been possible for them to go to the wrong tomb, then why did no-one explain their mistake when the disciples started preaching the resurrection? It would have made the disciples the laughing stock of Jerusalem when the authorities pointed out that they had in fact gone to Aunty Joan's tomb, and that Jesus' tomb was still there with Jesus' body inside!

Even supposing that they had, against all odds, gone to the wrong tomb, that still fails to explain the resurrection appearances. The claim was not simply that the tomb was empty, but that his followers had met the risen Jesus.

The body was stolen

The obvious question in response to the above is – by whom? The Roman and Jewish authorities would have had a vested interest in Jesus' body staying in the tomb. Certainly if they had moved it, possibly to a safer location, they would have been quick to produce the evidence as soon as the belief in Jesus' resurrection started to spread across the empire! And grave robbers would have had little reward for taking the body of a penniless preacher whose only possessions had been gambled over at his crucifixion. And why would a robber take the body but go to the trouble of leaving the grave clothes?

The most likely culprits would of course have been the disciples – but this explanation is also littered with problems. First, as we will see shortly, the disciples had not been expecting the resurrection to take place. Secondly, they would have had the small problem of making it past the Roman guard, placed there for that very purpose at pain of death. And had they somehow been able to do this, then there would have been a further problem: the disciples themselves would have known that the whole thing was a hoax. Not only would a hoax have been notoriously difficult to keep under wraps, but why did they continue to propagate the idea when they were losing their own lives for their beliefs?

The late Charles Colson who worked under the Nixon administration put it this way: 'Take it from one who was inside the Watergate web looking out, who saw first-hand how vulnerable a cover-up is: Nothing less than a witness as awesome as the resurrected Christ could have caused those men to maintain to their dying whispers that Jesus is alive and Lord.'[8]

The Bible itself shows that this idea was the first one put forward to account for the empty tomb: that the soldiers were paid to say that the disciples stole the body while they were sleeping.[9] Of course it begs the question of how they knew it was the disciples who had stolen the body, if in fact they were all asleep!

Again, such a view also fails to answer the other strands

of evidence. What are we to make of the resurrection appearances, for example?

Jesus' twin brother(!)

William Lane Craig mentions an event he attended in a university in California where he was debating on the subject of the resurrection. His opponent accepted the evidence surrounding the resurrection but still denied the actual event. His explanation was that Jesus had an identical twin brother who came to Jerusalem after the crucifixion and was mistaken for him! The problems with such a view are so obvious that they are laughable and hardly need stating. Why do we have no evidence of the twin brother? Why did the authorities not point out the body of the real Jesus – no doubt it was still lying in the tomb? Why did Jesus' twin not inform people of their mistake?

What these alternatives show us is that, while at first glance the claim of the resurrection seems ridiculous, once you start to take into account the historical material, it is the alternatives that appear more ridiculous. It may seem crazy to believe in the resurrection, but I find that, given what we now know, it would be even crazier to believe anything else.

Sir Lionel Luckhoo was hailed by *The Guinness Book of Records* as the world's most successful lawyer. His fame was such that *The Simpsons* even named a character after him (though, ironically, while the real-life Lionel almost never lost a case, his cartoon version never won one!). He stated, 'I say unequivocally the evidence for the resurrection of Jesus Christ is so overwhelming that it compels acceptance by proof which leaves absolutely no room for doubt.'[10]

Tom Wright, one of the world's leading biblical scholars, has taught at Cambridge and Oxford universities and is now a research professor at the University of St Andrews. He concludes, 'I have come to the conviction that the rise of the early church in the 40s and 50s is completely inexplicable, historically speaking, unless you have a strongly historical, bodily view of the resurrection of Jesus of Nazareth.'[11]

Still not convinced?

The biggest obstacle we will find as we come to the resurrection is not the historical evidence but our prior philosophical convictions. If you come to the investigation with the presupposition that God doesn't exist and miracles are impossible, then of course the resurrection too will seem impossible. But that would be a circular argument, of the type that Christians are often accused of employing. It's like saying that the football results must be wrong because your team have never lost, and would never lose, to those minnows. Well, maybe they just did! Any theory or presupposition needs to be open to being challenged by the available evidence. As one professor of law and humanities put it, 'The only way we can know whether an event can occur is to see whether in fact it has occurred. The problem of miracles, then, must be solved in the realm of historical investigation, not in the realm of philosophical speculation.'[12]

If believing in the resurrection still seems too big an intellectual and cultural leap for you to make, it is worth realizing that it would have been an even bigger one for the first followers of Jesus, but for different reasons. We may find that the idea of the resurrection doesn't fit with our presuppositions, but it didn't fit for them either. All of the original disciples were Jews. For a first-century Jew to have believed that God had lived as a human being on planet earth, had died a criminal's death at the hands of the Romans, only to rise again from the dead three days later, was no more part of their expectations than it is of ours. Jews did have a belief in resurrection, but this would occur at the end of time – not to one individual in the middle of history.

It is clear from the Gospel accounts that the disciples were not expecting the resurrection, in spite of Jesus' repeated statements that he would die and three days later rise again. You might expect that three days after the crucifixion they would be gathering together to see if the resurrection had happened yet. Not at all. For all we know, the men were still in bed and the women had gone to anoint what they thought was a dead body. They believed in the resurrection not because it was what they expected or because it was easy to believe, but because they were convinced it was true. They were willing to investigate the evidence and allow it to challenge their presuppositions of what they thought was possible. We too should do the same.

Sir Edward Clarke wrote, 'As a lawyer I have made a prolonged study of the evidences for the events of the first Easter Day. To me the evidence is conclusive, and over and over again in the High Court I have secured the verdict on evidence not nearly so compelling.'[13]

Too good to be true?

We have looked in the last few chapters at the hope the Bible gives. It may be tempting to think, 'Is it too good to be true?' Surely Christians only believe this stuff because they *want* it to be true. But the Christian hope is not 'too good to be true' – it is 'so good *because* it is true'.[14] It is not based on wishful thinking, but on a real historical event that we have been able to investigate. It is because of this that so many are able to face the future and death with such rock-solid confidence.

As I was writing these very words, I received news that

Dave, a good friend of mine and not much older than myself, had died. Although I knew he was dying, the speed of his passing was still a shock. I had been hoping to go and stay with him in a few weeks' time. There were so many things I now wish I had been able to say. So many memories will live on – the late-night chats, great meals together and the walks we enjoyed in the beautiful Lake District. I'm hit with the reality that he is gone. He won't ever walk into the room with his cheerful smile and familiar voice again.

I had heard from him a few weeks before. He knew he was going to die, and yet there was still a confidence in what he said. He knew where he was going. And it is this hope that gives me a sense of joy today, even through the tears. I know that for the Christian it is never really 'goodbye' but only ever '*au revoir*'. I will see my friend again. We will sit down again to enjoy great food and go for hikes. This hope is real. Because Jesus rose from the dead.

I first met Barry while working on a farm during my summer holidays as a student. He was married to Paula and they had two young children. A couple of years later, his wife was diagnosed with cancer. In spite of the treatment she received, her condition deteriorated, and very soon she died. At her funeral their small village church was packed with friends, family and neighbours. As they brought the coffin into the church, a song was played over the loudspeakers. It was Paula herself singing. Just a few weeks before, knowing that she would soon die, she had recorded words that summed up her confidence:

> No guilt in life, no fear in death,
> This is the power of Christ in me;
> From life's first cry to final breath,
> Jesus commands my destiny.

No power of hell, no scheme of man,
Can ever pluck me from his hand;
Till he returns, or calls me home,
Here in the power of Christ I'll stand.

(Extract taken from the song 'In Christ Alone' by Keith Getty and Stuart Townend, copyright © 2001 Thankyou Music*)

The hope Jesus gives is no pipe dream or illusion. It is not a mirage that cruelly disappoints upon arrival. It is real and true. Just as certainly as Jesus rose from the dead, so we can know that death is not the end. The best is yet to come.

Just as certainly as Jesus rose from the dead, so we can know that death is not the end. The best is yet to come.

At the end of *The Last Battle*, C. S. Lewis portrays the kind of hope that can be offered in the face of death:

Then Aslan turned to them and said: 'You do not yet look so happy as I mean you to be.'

Lucy said, 'We're so afraid of being sent away, Aslan. And you have sent us back into our own world so often.'

'No fear of that,' said Aslan. 'Have you not guessed?'

Their hearts leaped within and wild hope rose within them.

'There *was* a real railway accident,' said Aslan softly. 'Your father and mother and all of you are – as you used to call it in the Shadowlands – dead. The term is over: the holidays have begun. The dream is ended: this is the morning.'

And as He spoke He no longer looked to them like a lion; but the things that began to happen after that were so great and beautiful that I cannot write them. And for us this is the end of all the stories, and we can most truly say that they all lived happily ever after. But for them it was only the beginning of the real story. All their life in this world and all their adventures in Narnia had been only the cover and the title page: now at last they were beginning Chapter One of the Great Story which no one on earth has read: which goes on forever: in which every chapter is better than the one before.[15]

As we listen to such a mouth-watering description of the future, we may be tempted to ask, 'Why can't we go there now?' Why do we have to go on living here on earth?

8. WHY NOT NOW?

We have seen something of the amazing hope that Jesus offers the world: new bodies and restored relationships in a creation set free from decay and death. Also, this hope is no pipe dream based on wishful thinking, but rather a certain hope based on the resurrection of Jesus. Jesus is the one who has done everything necessary to bring this new world about. But why doesn't he just do it now? Why do we have to go on living in this broken world?

In some ways, we *can* start to experience that future now. For those who trust in Jesus, the work of new creation has already begun. As one Bible writer put it, 'Therefore, if anyone is in Christ, the new creation has come: the old has gone, the new is here!'[1]

What does that mean for us today? For a start, we can know and relate to God as a friend and grow in that relationship. We can also enjoy restored relationships with others. We may experience some degree of healing now from sickness. We've seen that our appreciation of the natural world can be enhanced. Just as we appreciate gifts even more when we know they come from someone we love, so we can enjoy this world now as a beautiful and creative gift from a good and loving God. There are real benefits to be had today from following Jesus.

Yet while it is possible to experience something of this new creation right now, in other ways it is still to come. We can know God personally, but we don't yet see him face to face. Life today is still like the engagement period, but we long for the wedding day. We enjoy restored and new relationships, but these are still hard work, and there is still the potential that we will get hurt or that we might hurt others. We may still get sick, and for many people, healing does not come right now. We can appreciate the natural world, but it can also be a harsh place in which to live.

The hope the Bible gives is partly realized here, but it is also yet to come. We still have to wait for the day when everything will be made new. But, to come back to the question, if Jesus has already shown that he has the power to bring about this new world, then why doesn't he do it right now? If through his death and resurrection he has made it possible, then why wait? Why do we have to go on living in this broken world with all its suffering and death? Every day more people suffer from lack of food. Women are raped. Children are abused. Millions live in fear and poverty. It may be that for you, life is really tough and every day is a battle. Why doesn't Jesus just sort it out once and for all?

Will it ever happen?
Will the hope that the Bible promises ever materialize? How can we really know that Jesus will deliver on his promises?

Might he have forgotten? Such questions are no surprise. They were anticipated 2,000 years ago:

> Above all, you must understand that in the last days scoffers will come, scoffing and following their own evil desires. They will say, 'Where is this "coming" he promised? Ever since our ancestors died, everything goes on as it has since the beginning of creation.' But they deliberately forget that long ago by God's word the heavens came into being and the earth was formed out of water and by water. By these waters also the world of that time was deluged and destroyed. By the same word the present heavens and earth are reserved for fire, being kept for the day of judgment and destruction of the ungodly.
>
> But do not forget this one thing, dear friends: with the Lord a day is like a thousand years, and a thousand years are like a day. The Lord is not slow in keeping his promise, as some understand slowness. Instead he is patient with you, not wanting anyone to perish, but everyone to come to repentance.
>
> But the day of the Lord will come . . .[2]

Peter, who wrote this letter, anticipated that in the future there would be people who would mock the very idea that the world would change. They would laugh at the very idea of a day of justice, and therefore think that they could carry on doing what they like here and now. Their mistake, says Peter, is that they forget that God already judged the world once and that he will do so again.

Picture the scene. You lived a very long time ago and were walking through some woods. A man with an axe is hacking down trees, and you stop to talk to him.

'What are you doing?' you ask.

'What does it look like?' he replies.

'Well, I can see what you're doing, but what are your plans for all this wood?'

'I'm building a boat,' he replies.

'A what?' you ask, never having heard of such a thing before.

He takes time to explain to you what a boat is and why you would want to use one. 'But why?' you ask. 'There's no water for miles around here.'

'Well, there isn't now,' he explains, 'but there soon will be. In fact, there is going to be a massive flood. God has said so. There is a day of judgment to come, and we need to be ready.'

By this point you aren't sure how to respond. He seems set on his course of action, even though it seems rather crazy, given the baking hot day and the dry and arid landscape all around.

Before long, others have taken notice of what is going on too. A crowd starts to gather, and after a few days it's all over the local news. At first some people take him seriously, but as time goes by they start to lose interest. The boat continues to be built, but there is still no sign of rain, let alone a flood.

Years pass, and people forget about the strange man with his boat-building project. Until, that is, you hear rumours that he has finished. Crowds gather to watch as he takes a whole zoo-load of animals into the boat along with his wife and kids. Some people are pointing and laughing at this seemingly ridiculous situation. One person shouts out, 'What are you doing? There'll be no flood! It's not even rai—'

He stops short. What no-one has noticed is that clouds have started to gather in the sky above. Just as he was speaking, the first large drop of rain fell and landed on the ground by his foot. The rest, as they say, is history.[3]

Peter tells us that, just as God judged the world once, so he will do it again. People may have mocked and laughed back then, but it did happen. People may laugh at the idea now, but it will still happen.

A day of justice

Of course, an ancient flood may seem like a far-fetched basis for believing in a future day of judgment. But the Bible also gives us a more recent and more verifiable event to base it on. Speaking in the city of Athens, the apostle Paul finished an address to the city's leading intellectual thinkers with these words:

> In the past God overlooked such ignorance, but now he commands all people everywhere to repent. For he has set a day when he will judge the world with justice by the man he has appointed. He has given proof of this to everyone by raising him from the dead.[4]

There will be a day of judgment, and the proof is the very event we discussed in the last chapter. It did happen and it will happen. The only problem is that, for many of us, the idea of judgment seems like a very negative thing. Why would we even want there to be such a day? Yet in the Bible, the Day of Judgment is seen as something to look forward to and rejoice in. Take these words from a song in the Old Testament:

> Let the heavens rejoice, let the earth be glad;
>   let the sea resound, and all that is in it.
> Let the fields be jubilant, and everything in them;
>   let all the trees of the forest sing for joy.
> Let all creation rejoice before the LORD, for he comes,
>   he comes to judge the earth.
> He will judge the world in righteousness
>   and the peoples in his faithfulness.[5]

Perhaps it would be easier to understand why this is a good idea, if we spoke not so much of a day of judgment, but of justice – for that is what judgment is meant to bring. The Bible says that there will be a day when justice is done, when wrong is put right and when evil is punished and defeated.

It will happen, no matter what people say. But why not now? The answer that Peter gives is not that God is slow or forgetful, but rather that he is patient. God longs to make the world new, but first he wants to make people new so that they can enjoy it. Yet as things stand, there are lots of people who would not be part of it. Many still insist on living their lives independently from God, refusing to receive the forgiveness and transformation he offers. God is patiently holding out the opportunity for people to come back to him and receive this hope.

It might be easy to read God's lack of intervention in this world as indifference on his part. Does he *really* care? Yet the answer is that he delays precisely because he *does* care. It is because he cares about us that he gives us another day in which to respond to him, receive his forgiveness and realize this hope. If you've not done anything about it yet, the main reason why God has given you today is so that you can do these very things.

So how should we respond?

We're told that God wants all people to come to repentance. 'Repentance' sounds like a religious word but it simply means to turn around or change direction. It's something I have to do repeatedly when driving in a new city. I recognize I have gone the wrong way and I turn around to go the right way.

The first thing we need to do then is turn around. We need to recognize that living life in independence from God

has not led to the real life that
we expected, but rather to the
exact opposite. In doing life our
own way, we have hurt God,
hurt others and made a mess
of his world. We haven't just
broken God's laws; we have broken his heart.

> *We haven't just
> broken God's laws;
> we have broken his
> heart.*

Secondly, we need to recognize our own powerlessness to sort out the mess we find ourselves in. The disciples couldn't sort out the storm; the citizens of the town couldn't help the demonized man; the doctors couldn't help the woman; and Jairus couldn't save his daughter. In the same way, we are powerless to bring about real and lasting change in ourselves, let alone in the world.

Thirdly, we need to trust in the one who can bring that change. Jesus, who calmed the storm, cured the man, healed the woman and raised the dead, is still able to change lives today. He has taken what we deserve on the cross. He made it possible for us to be forgiven and set free. He wants to forgive and change us, if we will only let him. We can trust him to change our lives now, and one day change the whole world into the way it ought to be.

The Bible says that the offer that Jesus gives is like an invitation to a party or a wedding. Have you replied to it yet? If not, what is stopping you from doing so today?

What's stopping you?

'It's too good to be true'
The hope the Bible gives may all seem like really good news, but you might still have a nagging doubt. Isn't it all just *too* good to be true? You don't want to buy into a delusion, no matter how good it seems. Remember what I quoted earlier,

that Christianity is not too good to be true; it is so good *because* it is true.[6] It is based on a rock-solid event in history that is both objective and verifiable. You can be confident and you can trust it.

'If it's true, then why doesn't everyone believe it?'

As I said earlier, most people that I meet haven't rejected Christianity because they have investigated it and found the evidence lacking. They have not investigated it in the first place. Don't judge Christianity based on other people's ignorance, but on what you have discovered for yourself.

Of course, some people do investigate it and still reject it. But is that because the evidence is unconvincing or because they are unwilling to admit that they need to turn around and trust Jesus? While trusting Jesus is a really simple thing, it is also a humbling thing because it means that we have to admit that we've been wrong all along. Frankly, it's not so much a case that some people can't believe, but that they won't believe.

'I've got lots more questions'

More questions? Great! Christianity has nothing to fear from questions. Because it is true and based on objective events in history, it opens itself up for questions and investigation in ways that other religions just can't. As we ask our questions and investigate the answers, we can grow in our confidence that it's true. But you don't need to wait till every question has been answered before you can make a decision. Based on what you now know, what would be more reasonable: to reject Christianity as rubbish or to believe it? Which would be a bigger leap: to trust Jesus for yourself or write it off as fantasy?

'I've got stuff to sort out first'

Many people think they need to sort out their lives before they come to Jesus. But why try to sort it out on your own? We are powerless really to sort our lives out, but Jesus specializes in it – he has been doing it for a long time now! We can simply bring him the mess and the rubbish, and not only let him forgive us but start to change us too.

'What will other people think?'

The worry about how other people will respond can be a major barrier, and this is not necessarily without basis. Sometimes people may reject us if we say that we have started to follow Jesus, but if there is one thing that would be worth losing anything for, it is this. Following Jesus shouldn't make us a worse friend or spouse, but a better one, as we experience Jesus' love and so love others differently as a result. Any friend worthy of the name would stick by you, even if they didn't at first fully understand what you have done.

'But my friends and family aren't Christians . . .'

If your friends and family aren't Christians, this doesn't need to stop you from being the first to discover Jesus. In fact, you could well be the very means by which they come to discover him too.

So why not now?

It may be that you realize that you have never responded to Jesus' invitation, but you would like to and know that you need to. The best way to do something about it is simply to talk to God. Tell him how you feel and what you would like to do. The words of the following prayer may be helpful:

Dear God,

I'm really sorry for living my own way.
I'm sorry I've so often ignored you and done my own thing.
I recognize that this has not only hurt other people, but it also
hurt you.
I know I can't sort it out on my own and I need you.

Thank you that Jesus can do what I can't.
Thank you that he came to put things right.
Thank you that he died and took the hell that I deserved.
Thank you that because of what he did, I can be forgiven and
brought back into a relationship with you.

Please will you forgive me and come into my life right now and
change me?
Help me to live my life with you right at the centre of it.
Please give me this hope that one day you will put all
things right.
Please make this hope real for me so I can look forward
to it today.

I ask this in the name of Jesus,

Amen.

If you have responded to the invitation, then let me say,
'Congratulations!' This is the best decision you will ever
make and the start of an adventure. It won't always be easy,
but it will certainly be worth it.

So what difference does following Jesus make to your life
now? How does having this hope for the future change the
way you live today?

9. IT MAKES ALL THE DIFFERENCE IN THIS WORLD – AND THE NEXT

I wonder if you remember auditioning for the orchestra or a part in a play at school. It was a nerve-racking ordeal. You had to perform certain things to a satisfactory standard so that you could be accepted. The song or the speech might not have been the same as the one you finally performed. It was simply a test to see how good you were.

Rehearsal or audition?

For many religious people, life in this present world can be seen rather like an audition. We have a series of tests to pass in order to make the grade. If we do well and keep the rules, then one day we will get to go somewhere really nice. If we fail, then we will be punished. However, the things we do today may bear no similarity to what we will do in the future. Morality, for example, can ultimately seem rather arbitrary. For instance, in Islam it is forbidden to drink alcohol. Yet the Qur'an says that, in paradise, there will be rivers of wine

to be enjoyed.[1] In this instance, you forgo something today
in the hope that you can have lots of it later! Such laws can
seem rather random and lead to the idea that religious living
involves a suppression of our natural desires and a negative
way of life.

A rehearsal is, however, quite different from an audition.
Here you are not performing in the hope of being accepted,
as in an audition, but you know that you already have been
accepted. In this instance, you practise hard because you
know that what you are doing today you will do one day for
real on stage.

The Christian life is much more like a rehearsal than an
audition. There is no test for us to pass. Jesus has already
met God's entry requirements and done everything we
need. We need not fear rejec-
tion or failure if we trust him.
Life today is not an audition
for heaven, but a rehearsal for
life on the new earth. Because
there is continuity between
today and the future, what we
do today is not arbitrary. We
are to start living today in the way that we will do for all
eternity.

We are to start living
today in the way
that we will do for all
eternity.

Everything matters

We are to live for the future, but it is important to remember
what kind of future we are waiting for. Some people might
think that living for the future means only being interested in
supposedly 'spiritual' things: singing songs, reading the Bible,
going to church and evangelizing others. All other activities
can be regarded as ultimately pointless – like rearranging
deckchairs on the *Titanic*.

If Christian hope was just about going to heaven, then this might well be true. However, as we have seen, our hope is for a renewed world and renewed bodies. That means that what we do in this present world, with these bodies, matters. Our future involves real relationships, with others and with God, so those relationships matter right now. Because God will redeem everything, everything matters. We should not divide the 'spiritual' and the 'physical'. Such a view totally changes the way we should live today, but not so that we live detached from the world around us. Rather, having this hope should lead us to be more involved in this world and to enjoy it even more. How can this be? Let's summarize some of the different aspects of that hope and see how they can affect us today.

Relationship to our environment

We have seen that our physical world is not going to be destroyed, but renewed and transformed. Nothing good will be lost. What does that mean for us today?

Firstly, we can really enjoy this world. In fact, God wants us to enjoy it – that's why he made it. This world is a gift from him, to be enjoyed in relationship with him. Knowing the giver means that we can enjoy his gift even more than we would have done before. Jesus said, 'I have come that [you] may have life, and have it to the full.'[2] So, as I ski down the stunning Austrian Alps or cycle through the New Forest on a midsummer evening, my enjoyment is enhanced because I know the one who made it all. He is not like a disapproving boss looking down on me, waiting for me to get back to work. Rather, he is a kind father who delights in the enjoyment that one of his children can have of the gifts he has given.

Enjoying God's world doesn't just mean going for nice

walks on a Sunday afternoon. It means enjoying the richness
and diversity of this world. This can involve playing sport,
eating great food, drinking fine wine, watching a film or
going to the theatre. It could mean studying the sciences or
developing a love of art. We might learn to paint, take great
photographs or write beautiful music. Gardening, cooking
or writing computer programmes can all be part of making
the most of life in this world.

But while we are able to enjoy everything that is good, we
are also freed from the need to do everything right now. If
I don't get to swim the Great Barrier Reef in this life, that's
OK. I won't miss out. It will be even better in the future.
Some people can spend all their retirement years and life
savings trying to see as many places as possible before it's too
late. But it's never too late. It's not that it's wrong to enjoy
lovely holidays – quite the opposite. But we are also free to
forgo some of those things and use our time and money for
other worthy purposes.

Not only should we enjoy this world, but we should also
look after it. Environmental concern would seem like a
waste of time if the world is just going to be destroyed. But
knowing that it will last forever means that we should take
good care of it. Caring for creation was the first task God
gave to human beings, and it's still a task today.

Relationships with one another

I am aware that you may be feeling the pain of a broken
relationship even as you read this. Relationships carry the
potential for the greatest joy in life but also the deepest pain.
Broken relationships can take years to heal and, sadly, sometimes they never do. And the painful reality we all face is that
ultimately every relationship is broken by death.

Yet, as we've seen, this doesn't have to be the end. We

will not enjoy God's new world on our own. We won't be living individualistic lives in some private paradise, devoid of contact with other people. Nor will it be some kind of monastic experience where nothing but prayer is allowed. Relationships, such a valuable part of life today, will be central to our enjoyment of life one day.

So what difference does that make today? For a start, we will realize that people matter. Our society has a tendency to love things (such as computers, cars, gadgets) and use people. By contrast, we should love people and use things. We can be tempted to gossip at work and tear people down with our words. Instead, we'll want to build others up and encourage them wherever we can.

It also means that *all* people matter, whoever they are. We can end up respecting and wanting to hang out with those who are regarded as significant, successful or beautiful in this world's eyes. But in God's new world there will be a radical reordering. Some of those who seemed so successful and significant in this present world will not even be part of it. Others who were neglected or rejected by society will come to prominence. C. S. Lewis conveyed this idea well in his book *The Great Divorce*. Here he introduces us to different individuals in the life to come. He shows how some people who are currently outwardly very attractive are inwardly quite ugly. There are others who would never receive a second look, but they are actually very beautiful people. In the future, their outward appearance will reflect their inner state.

This means practically that we should care about those whom no-one else has time for. In the past, this meant that Christians worked sacrificially to abolish the slave trade, provide free education and hospital care for all, and stand up for the rights of those who had no voice. Having this hope means that we will value those whom others might despise. For some people I know, this means working with the 'untouchables' of India, and for others, with the street kids in South America. For us, it might start by changing our attitude to the elderly widow next door. All people, whoever they are, do matter.

We should also value and invest in relationships. Sometimes the pain of broken relationships can, naturally, cause us to be guarded about building new ones. Yet, though death has separated me from good friends, I know that I will see some of them again. Our relationships matter and will be continued. All is not lost.

One of the best places to see how Jesus can restore relationships is in the church. As an establishment, the church can receive a lot of bad press, and this is not always without reason. Sadly, many churches have moved far away from Jesus and what the Bible actually teaches. For some, this means that they aren't really churches, as the Bible would describe them, at all.

But there are many other churches made up of people who genuinely love Jesus: a group of people who have been changed by him and are looking forward with hope to the future. That, after all, is what a church is – not a building or an organization, but a group of ordinary people, united in their love for Jesus.

I have travelled all over the world, and in each country I have met communities of Christians united in their love for God and for one another. I don't think there is anywhere else in society where you would find such a diverse group of people. My home church consists of people from different age groups, countries and classes of society. We have individuals with different political persuasions and very different jobs. There is nothing that would naturally bring such a group together. Yet it is not simply that we sit in the same building for an hour each week, but this group of people really do love one another. Elderly people spend time with students and cook them dinner. Grandparents give advice to young mums. High wage-earners sit down to discuss the Bible with the unemployed. People share their possessions to help others. In so many ways, it can feel like family, which is exactly what it is meant to be. If your experience of church has been negative, then don't give up.

But why is the church so special? What is it that makes these relationships so strong? Some people might view the church a little bit like a lifeboat. It's useful to rescue you from a dying world, but there's little value in getting to know the other people in the boat – after all, you won't be together for very long. Others may see it as the place where they go on their own to meet with God. Some don't even go to a church but stay at home to watch bigger churches on the internet or on TV. We can judge churches like a consumer, by the quality of the music and the preaching.

But the church is not just a lifeboat, nor is it a show that helps me to connect with God. It is not a music concert or a preaching centre. It is, at its heart, a new community of people who are going to spend eternity together in God's new world. Those relationships matter today because they are going to last forever. Of course, some might dread the very thought of spending eternity with the members of their local church. It's good to remember that in the future they will be perfect, and so they will be a whole lot less annoying. The same will be true of us too!

So if a church is not just a useful place to help you get to heaven in good shape, but made up of the very people who are going to spend eternity together, it's really important not so much to go to a church, but to be a *part* of a church. Find a lively one that teaches the Bible and where people quite obviously love Jesus and one another too.

Relationship with God

Coming to trust Jesus means beginning a relationship with God. In some ways, as we have already noted, it may seem like a long-distance one – we can't actually see God. However, we do have his presence with us: he promises to give us the Holy Spirit, his unseen self, to live with and in us. The Bible describes the relationship of a Christian to God as being like that of a bride to her bridegroom. It is one of love, joy and intimacy. Life is the engagement period; the Bible says that there is a wedding day yet to come. In fact, one of the most popular pictures of the future in the Bible is of a wedding celebration.

Our greatest joy in the age to come will be knowing God, personally and intimately. It is from him that all the other wonderful gifts come. If the gifts are so good, then how good must the giver be? All beauty, goodness and love come from him, for he is beautiful, good, and the source of all love. The beauty that we see in creation is a reflection of his great beauty. Everything good that we enjoy in this world comes from his great goodness. All the love that we share with others is but an overflow of his incredible love. Getting to know this God could never be boring or dull. It is the greatest adventure of all.

So what does this mean for us today? I mentioned earlier that my brother is married to a Canadian and that, before they got married, they had a very long-distance relationship. I remember him coming home one day and announcing that they were going to get married. The date had been set. There was just a year to wait. So what did my brother do? Well, with the wedding all sorted, he realized he didn't need to worry about speaking to his fiancée any more. After all, if they were going to spend the rest of their lives together, they should make the most of their independence and freedom. So after a year of not talking, they finally got married.

Actually, as you've probably guessed, that's not what happened at all. Such a situation would be ridiculous. Knowing that the wedding day is coming is an incentive to speak to the one you love even more, not less! Of course, it was not as good as being married, but they wanted to invest in growing their relationship together.

If the greatest joy of the future will be knowing God, then one of our greatest pleasures today will be getting to know him better. Like any relationship, getting to know God better takes good communication. The Bible is primarily the way in which he speaks to us, and prayer is our way of talking to him.

Bible reading is not a ritual to earn God's acceptance any more than reading a love letter would earn my girlfriend's love! When we read the Bible, we're not looking primarily for what we need to do, but finding out what God has already done. We discover more and more what he is like. My main aim in reading the Bible is to discover how amazing God is, so that my heart is excited afresh by him.

In prayer we get to speak with God. This was never intended to be a formal or showy thing. In fact, Jesus condemned those who prayed to win the approval of others. We don't need to use special language, go through rituals or be in any particularly special place. God longs to hear us speak to him. We can thank him for what he has already done for us, as well as talk to him about the things that concern us. We can bring him our requests or just enjoy talking to him about what we are doing.

Just as in any relationship, it is good to factor in quality time with God. Many people find it helpful to have at least some time each day set aside to talk to God and listen to him as they read the Bible. But communication doesn't have to be limited to a set time. I love meditating on a verse of the Bible as I drive along or simply saying 'thank you' to God for a great meal, a beautiful sunset or a wonderful evening with friends. Each morning, I thank God not only that the sun has risen, but that Jesus has risen and defeated darkness and given us light. Every year as winter turns to spring, I am reminded that death has been defeated and there is new life to come.

The future begins today

Living for the future means learning to live in this present world, as we will do forever. One day the world will be transformed, and so will we, if we are trusting in Jesus. Finally we will be free, even from the temptation to do wrong things. We will truly be the people we were created to be.

I remember a friend of mine telling me that, in the future, after God has made everything new, the greatest compliment you will pay someone will be this: 'You haven't changed much!' Don't misunderstand me. I'm not talking about our physical bodies. While I think we will still be recognizable, just as Jesus was, our bodies will be changed. They will be freed from decay and death, never to die again. That will be a radical change and one that I am really looking forward to. But what about the person I am on the inside? My attitudes, thoughts and the way I treat others? I am to become increasingly today what I will be forever. God will one day finish that work, but he wants to start it today, making me into the person I was always meant to be.

The ultimate happy ending

I have referred several times to C. S. Lewis's Narnia books and J. R. R. Tolkien's *The Lord of the Rings*. What often surprises people is that, while *The Lord of the Rings* was popularly regarded as the best work of fiction in the twentieth century, it was originally rejected by many literary critics. In fact, even today with its massive success, it fares little better. One of the criticisms of the book is that it has a happy ending. Evil is finally defeated. Critics protest that this is not true to life where there is ultimately no happy ending. We find that we love the stories that have happy endings, but can become cynical about the possibility because we think that life is not really like that. When you reject the Christian story, you end up rejecting all other stories with happy endings, for we think that no such ending can exist. But when you accept the Christian story, you learn not only to love and appreciate it, but also every other story, for we know that life really is like that.

Both Tolkien and Lewis wrote great stories because they believed the greatest story of all. They could paint a happy ending because they knew that ultimately there would be one. Nearly all of our films and novels tell the same story. They begin with a state of equilibrium: things are relatively good. But then something goes wrong, and there seems to be no hope. Just when all seems lost, someone steps in to rescue the situation and to save the day. By the end, it is not simply that the original state is restored, but it is even better. The reason we love

We feel this world is broken because it is. We long for someone to rescue us and he has. We look forward to a day when things will be put right – and they will be.

these fictional stories so much is because they are echoes of the true story.

We feel this world is broken because it is. We long for someone to rescue us and he has. We look forward to a day when things will be put right – and they will be.

There is a day coming. There is hope. It is real.

One of my favourite Christian songs sums up this hope well:

There is a day
That all creation's waiting for,
A day of freedom and liberation for the earth.
And on that day
The Lord will come to meet His bride,
And when we see Him
In an instant we'll be changed.

The trumpet sounds
And the dead will then be raised
By His power,
Never to perish again.
Once only flesh,
Now clothed with immortality,
Death has now been
Swallowed up in victory.

So lift your eyes
To the things as yet unseen,
That will remain now
For all eternity.
Though trouble's hard,
It's only momentary

And it's achieving
Our future glory.

We will meet Him in the air
And then we will be like Him,
For we will see Him as He is.
Then all hurt and pain will cease
And we'll be with Him forever
And in His glory we will live.

(From 'There Is a Day' by Nathan Fellingham, copyright © 2001
Thankyou Music*)

APPENDIX

Destruction or redemption – what will happen to this world?

What is the future for our world? Environmental disaster, nuclear meltdown or a meteorite collision? Throughout this book I have explained that the Bible says that it is none of these things. This world is not going to be destroyed. God loves it and cares for it too much to let that happen. Redemption, not destruction, is the future for our world. But that's not what some Christians have thought. Some point to a particular passage in the New Testament that seems to suggest that it will be destroyed:

> But the day of the Lord will come like a thief. The heavens will disappear with a roar; the elements will be destroyed by fire, and the earth and everything done in it will be laid bare.
>
> Since everything will be destroyed in this way, what kind of people ought you to be? You ought to live holy and godly lives as you look forward to the day of God and speed its coming. That day will bring about the destruction of the heavens by

fire, and the elements will melt in the heat. But in keeping
with his promise we are looking forward to a new heaven and
a new earth, where righteousness dwells.

So then, dear friends, since you are looking forward to this,
make every effort to be found spotless, blameless and at peace
with him.[1]

At first reading, this passage appears to give the impression
that everything is going to be destroyed. Some Christians
have even suggested that it is describing the effects of a
nuclear war. But there are a few things that we need to bear
in mind.

Firstly, what does it mean by the 'elements' that are going
to be destroyed? This word reminds me of chemistry lessons
and having to learn the periodic table. 'Elements' can mean
the building blocks of the world – the stuff that it is made
out of. However, I don't think that is what is being described
here. Elsewhere in the New Testament when this same word
is used, it clearly does not refer to the physical elements that
make up our world, but rather to the spiritual forces of evil
that hold the world captive.[2] So it would appear that it is not
the world that is going to be destroyed (which would contradict other parts of the Bible that we have already looked at),
but rather it is evil that will be done away with.

Secondly, when Peter writes about a new heaven and a
new earth, he doesn't mean *brand* new – in the sense that
the old ones cease to exist. 'New' can also mean 'renewed',
just as we would speak about a new moon. It seems that
when the Bible mentions the new earth, it does so in this
latter sense. It will be the same earth, but made new and
transformed.

Finally, it is worth remembering that this passage comes
straight after the one we looked at in chapter 8 regarding the

Old Testament flood. Did the flood destroy the world? Yes and no. It was a flood of judgment but also of purification. The world after the flood was still the same world. In the same way, the fire spoken of here is one both of judgment *and* refining. Just as you might use fire to refine gold by burning the dross, so the coming fire burns up the rubbish, leaving what is good, pure and precious.

C. S. Lewis captures this well in *The Last Battle*. As we have already seen, the children think that Narnia has been destroyed, but they find themselves in a new world that they realize is the same as the old Narnia they have just left, and yet it is even better than before. The Lord Digory (who many believe is Lewis's portrayal of himself) explains, 'You need not mourn over Narnia, Lucy. All of the old Narnia that mattered, all the dear creatures, have been drawn into the real Narnia through the Door. And of course it is different; as different as a real thing is from a shadow or as waking life is from a dream.'[3]

Nothing good from this world will be lost. In the penultimate chapter of the Bible we are told, regarding this new earth, that 'the kings of the earth will bring their splendour into it'.[4] Everything worth keeping will be kept, cleaned up and made even better. The glorious beauty of the Alps or the staggering colours of the Great Barrier Reef will be a part of it. We will be able to enjoy Beethoven, Bach and Mozart or something more modern if we don't like classical music! Art and architecture, parks and gardens, literature and poetry will not be destroyed but redeemed. The skills we gained, the learning we acquired, the relationships we built and the people we have become will not be destroyed but preserved and continued.

Such a hope really does affect how you live today.

NOTES

Introduction

1 John Mayer, 'Waiting on the World to Change', from the album *Continuum*, 2006.

2 I am indebted to Timothy Keller for this illustration.

3 Quoted in http://www.gadflyonline.com/11-5-01/art-bacon. html.

4 Bertrand Russell, *A Free Man's Worship*, http://www. philosophicalsociety.com/Archives/A%20Free%20Man's%20 Worship.htm.

5 Bertrand Russell, *The Autobiography of Bertrand Russell*, vol. 2 (Little Brown & Co., 1968), pp. 95–96.

6 Sam Sparro, 'Black and Gold', from the album *Sam Sparro*, 2008.

7 Richard Dawkins, *The God Delusion* (Bantam Press, 2006), p. 288.

Chapter 1: What are you waiting for?

1 Cecil Francis Alexander, 'Once in Royal David's City', 1848.

2 If you want to look more into how we can know the Bible is true, then I recommend: Amy Orr-Ewing, *Why Trust the Bible?* (IVP, 2005) and Lee Strobel, *The Case for Christ* (Zondervan, 1998).

3 Romans 8:18–25.

4 See 1 Corinthians 15:20–23. Here Jesus' resurrection is described

as being the 'firstfruits'. In biblical times, the first fruits of the harvest were the indication that more was on the way. In the same way, Jesus' resurrection is seen as the first of many that will one day follow.

5 It is true that there are two occasions where people fail to recognize Jesus after the resurrection. The first is where Mary mistakes him for a gardener. But a closer reading reveals that she wasn't looking directly at Jesus when she assumed this and she was blinded by her tears. When she hears Jesus' voice and turns to him, she is in no doubt as to who he is (John 20:11–16). On the other occasion (Luke 24:13–35), we are told that the two disciples are prevented from understanding who Jesus is. It seems the miracle here is not that they recognize Jesus, but rather that for the first part they don't. On all other occasions, people do recognize Jesus.

6 Joni Eareckson Tada, *Heaven: Your Real Home* (Zondervan, 1995), p. 53.

7 2 Peter 3:13.

8 C. S. Lewis, *The Last Battle* (HarperCollins, 2001), pp. 203–205.

9 Ibid., pp. 206–207.

10 Vinoth Ramachandra, *The Scandal of Jesus* (IVP, 2001), p. 24.

11 *The Lord of the Rings: The Two Towers*, directed by Peter Jackson, New Line Cinema, 2002.

12 Romans 8:18.

Chapter 2: What's wrong with this world?

1 Aleksandr Solzhenitsyn, *The Gulag Archipelago* (Collins, 1974), p. 168.

2 The idea of God creating the world is often ridiculed as mythical. Yet historically, among Christians, there have been different ways of reading these early chapters in Genesis. This is partly because they appear to be unique as a literary genre, unrepeated elsewhere in the Bible. Therefore some read them

in a very literal sense, others in a more poetic way. Some reckon that Genesis excludes any possibility of evolution, while others synchronize the two. Since becoming a Christian, I have changed my mind on this several times while still remaining a Christian. You don't need to come to one particular opinion on this to become a Christian. But despite differences in how we read these early chapters, all Christians would agree that they teach us some foundational things about the world in which we live.

3 Genesis 2:18.

4 The *Daily Telegraph*, 19 June 2009.

5 See Genesis 3:8.

6 Genesis 3:1–9.

7 Genesis 3:12.

8 Genesis 3:16.

9 Genesis 3:19.

10 Richard Dawkins, *River Out of Eden: A Darwinian View of Life* (Phoenix, 1995), p. 133.

11 Richard Dawkins, *The God Delusion* (Black Swan, 2007), p. 253.

12 Oliver Sacks, *Awakenings* (Picador, 1991), pp. 28–29.

13 Quoted from a talk.

14 Cited by Amy Orr-Ewing in http://www.bethinking.org/ truth-tolerance/beginner/dont-all-religions-lead-to-god.htm.

15 John Gray, *Black Mass* (Penguin, 2008), p. 11.

Chapter 3: Back to the future I

1 Isaiah 2:2–4.

2 Isaiah 11:6–9.

3 Mark 4:35–41.

4 See Psalm 107:29.

5 See Richard Bauckham, *Jesus and the Eyewitnesses* (Eerdmans, 2008).

6 See Paul Barnett, *Is the New Testament Reliable?* (IVP, 2005).

7 For an extended look at the subject of miracles and, in particular, whether miracles contradict the laws of nature, I recommend C. S. Lewis, *Miracles* (HarperCollins, 2002).

8 See Luke 13:1–5.

9 From the sermon 'Weight of Glory', available online at http://www.verber.com/mark/xian/weight-of-glory.pdf.

Chapter 4: Back to the future II

1 Mark 5:1–20.

2 G. K. Chesterton, *What's Wrong with the World?* (Cassell and Co., 1910), p. 39.

3 In their 2006 report 'Truth Hurts', The Camelot Foundation and Mental Health Foundation say that evidence suggests the UK has the highest rate of self-harm in Europe, http://www.samaritans.org/media_centre/emotional_health_news/epidemic-self-harm-033.aspx.

4 http://www.rcpsych.ac.uk/mentalhealthinfo/mentalhealthandgrowingup/self-harminyoungpeople/michellesstory.aspx.

5 John Mayer, 'Gravity', from the album *Continuum*, 2008.

6 Quoted from a talk by Michael Reeves.

7 Quoted in the *Daily Telegraph*, 13 January 2012, http://blogs.telegraph.co.uk/news/tomchiversscience/100122576/on-larry-king-and-an-atheists-fear-of-death/.

Chapter 5: Back to the future III

1 Woody Allen, *Without Feathers* (Ballantine Books, 1983), p. 106.

2 Quoted in http://www.people.com/people/article/0,,1147497,00.html.

3 http://blogs.telegraph.co.uk/news/tomchiversscience/100122576/on-larry-king-and-an-atheists-fear-of-death/.

4 *Third Way*, December 2011.

5 *Q* Magazine, November 2006.
6 Mark 5:21–43.
7 Revelation 21:4.
8 J. R. R. Tolkien, *The Lord of the Rings* (HarperCollins, 1995), p. 930.
9 In his song 'Imagine', from the album *Imagine*, 1971.

Chapter 6: All hell breaks loose
1 C. S. Lewis, *The Last Battle* (HarperCollins, 2001), p. 207.
2 Matthew 27:27–54.
3 2 Corinthians 5:19 NASB.
4 Luke 23:41.
5 Luke 23:42.
6 Luke 23:43.

Chapter 7: Wishful thinking?
1 John Gray, *Black Mass* (Penguin, 2008), p. 9.
2 Luke 24:18–21.
3 1 Corinthians 15:12–19.
4 Pinchas Lapide, *The Resurrection of Jesus: A Jewish Perspective* (Augsburg Fortress, 1983).
5 http://richarddawkins.net/audio/2834-conversation-between-richard-dawkins-and-john-lennox.
6 http://www.reasonablefaith.org/site/News2?page=NewsArticle&id=5351.
7 Geza Vermes, *Jesus the Jew: A Historian's Reading of the Gospels* (Collins, 1973), p. 39.
8 Charles Colson, *Loving God* (Marshalls, 1984), p. 69.
9 Matthew 28:11–15.
10 www.hawaiichristiansonline.com.
11 N. T. Wright, *The New Heavens and New Earth* (Grove, 1999), p. 4.
12 John Warwick Montgomery, *Where Is History Going?* (Bethany Fellowship, 1967), p. 71.

13   Sir Edward Clarke to E. L. Macassey, quoted in John Stott, *Basic Christianity*, 3rd edn (IVP, 2008), p. 58.

14   From a talk by Richard Cunningham.

15   C. S. Lewis, *The Last Battle* (HarperCollins, 2001), pp. 221–222.

Chapter 8: Why not now?

1   2 Corinthians 5:17.

2   2 Peter 3:3–10.

3   To read the whole original story, see Genesis 6 – 8.

4   Acts 17:30–31.

5   Psalm 96:11–15.

6   From a talk by Richard Cunningham.

Chapter 9: It makes all the difference in this world – and the next

1   Surah 47:15.

2   John 10:10.

Appendix: Destruction or redemption – what will happen to this world?

1   2 Peter 3:10–14.

2   The word 'elements' is also used in Galatians 4:3, 9; Colossians 2:8, 20 where it clearly refers to evil spiritual forces opposed to God's kingdom.

3   C. S. Lewis, *The Last Battle* (HarperCollins, 2001), p. 206.

4   Revelation 21:24.

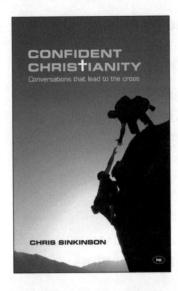

related titles from IVP

I'd Like To Believe, But …

Michael Green
& Nick Spencer

ISBN: 978-1-84474-390-2
144 pages, paperback

'Religious people are too intolerant.' 'You can't trust what is in the Bible.' 'Science has disproved Christianity.' 'There's too much suffering in the world.' 'Something 2,000 years ago can't be relevant to me today.'

Michael Green has responded to each of these statements in a direct and informal way, giving his Christian perspective on the opinions expressed. His easy style engages readers and shows how the Bible and Christian beliefs can provide a real faith for life. This book may even help you believe in spite of your buts …

'Based on real questions from real people in the real world. I would recommend this book to anyone investigating what Christianity is all about, and, as ever from Michael Green, it's brilliant stuff!' Andy Hawthorne

'Michael Green pulls no punches as he answers the voices of modern unbelief with love, humour and the power of Scripture-based scholarship. Authentic on both sides, the contrast makes compelling reading.' Jonathan Aitken

Available from your local Christian bookshop or **www.thinkivp.com**

related titles from IVP

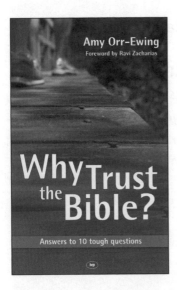

Why Trust the Bible?
Answers to 10 tough questions
Amy Orr-Ewing

ISBN: 978-1-84474-347-6
144 pages, paperback

'You don't honestly believe all that stuff in the Bible!'

Challenged by her friends, and later as a student by theological staff, Amy Orr-Ewing was determined to leave no stone unturned in her eagerness to prove that the Bible was unique and wholly reliable. Her passion drove her to complete an in-depth study of the answers to ten of the most frequently raised objections she encountered. Sensitively yet convincingly, the author addresses the arguments.

'This excellent book confronts ten difficult questions about the Bible with honesty and conviction, and will be invaluable to anyone wrestling with these questions.' Alister McGrath

'Brilliant! Amy's fascinating, wise and informative comments impressively counter much of the superficial and frequently unchallenged debunking of the Bible that we meet everywhere today.' Greg Haslam

'Amy is one of the foremost British evangelists and apologists of our generation.' Nicky Gumbel

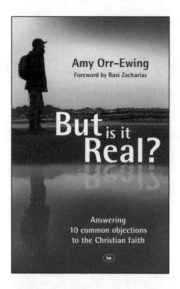